# COMPUTING MADE S

CW00370377

## AT ONLY £8.99 · 16

# Windows 3.1
# Made Simple

P.K.McBride

MADE SIMPLE
BOOKS

Made Simple
An imprint of Butterworth-Heinemann
Linacre House, Jordan Hill, Oxford OX2 8DP
225 Wildwood Avenue, Woburn, MA 01801-2041
A division of Reed Educational and Professional Publishing Ltd

ℛ  A member of the Reed Elsevier plc group

OXFORD   BOSTON   JOHANNESBURG
MELBOURNE   NEW DELHI   SINGAPORE

First published 1994
Reprinted 1994, 1995 (twice), 1996, 1997 (three times), 1998

**British Library Cataloguing in Publication Data**
A catalogue record for this book is available from the British Library

ISBN 0 7506  2072 2

🐫 Typeset by P.K.McBride, Southampton
Archtype, Bash Casual, Cotswold and Gravity fonts from Advanced Graphics Ltd
Icons designed by Sarah Ward © 1994
Printed and bound in Great Britain
by Scotprint, Musselburgh, Scotland

# Contents

# Preface

The computer is about as simple as a spacecraft, and who ever let an untrained spaceman loose? You pick up a manual that weighs more than your birth-weight, open it and find that its written in computerspeak. You see messages on the screen that look like code and the thing even makes noises. No wonder that you feel it's your lucky day if everything goes right. What do you do if everything goes wrong? Give up.

Training helps. Being able to type helps. Experience helps. This book helps, by providing training and assisting with experience. It can't help you if you always manage to hit the wrong keys, but it can tell you which are the right ones and what to do when you hit the wrong ones. After some time, even the dreaded manual will start to make sense, just because you know what the writers are wittering on about.

Computing is not black magic. You don't need luck or charms, just a bit of understanding. The problem is that the programs that are used nowadays look simple but aren't. Most of them are crammed with features you don't need – but how do you know what you don't need? This book shows you what is essential and guides you through it. You will know how to make an action work and why. The less essential bits can wait – and once you start to use a program with confidence you can tackle these bits for yourself.

The writers of this series have all been through it. We know your time is valuable, and you don't want to waste it. You don't buy books on computer subjects to read jokes or be told that you are a dummy. You want to find what you need and be shown how to achieve it. Here, at last, you can.

# 1 Essentials

# The jargon

## Windows

The system that provides an easy interface between the computer and you. It consists of a central core that organises the whole shebang and a set of programs offering a wide range of facilities.

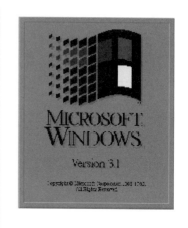

## Window

An area of the screen that displays the activities of a program. Its size and position can be changed at any time. One program may run several windows, each handling a different aspect of its work, and windows from different programs may be open at the same time. Whichever one you are working on will be on the top.

## Pointer

Also called the **Cursor** - for locating items on screen. Its appearance varies with the activity.

## Icons

These are small images. The commonest are:

- **Program icons** – programs in the Program Manager window or ones that have been shrunk down out of the way.

- **Window icons** – open windows that have been shrunk down out of the way.

- **Command icons** – a quick way of giving commands. They are used in many Windows programs.

| File | Options | Window | Help |
|------|---------|--------|------|
| New... | | | |
| Open | | Enter | |
| Move... | | F7 | |
| Copy... | | F8 | |
| Delete | | Del | |
| Properties... | | Alt+Enter | |
| Run... | | | |
| Exit Windows... | | | |

# Menus

Lists of commands. Most programs will show 6 or more names at the top of the window in a **menu bar**. Selecting the name pulls down a menu of command options. Some menus will have a second level of sub-menus opening up from them. (See Making choices, page 12.)

# Application

Software designed for the end-user, as opposed to that which the system uses directly. Spread-sheets, word-processors, databases, desktop publishing packages and games are typical applications.

# The screen

What you see on screen when you start Windows depends upon how it was set up and how you left it last time. And, of course, what the screen looks like once you are into your working session, is infinitely variable. Having said that, there are certain basic principles that always apply and certain things which are always there. It is the fact that all Windows applications share a common approach that makes Windows such an easy system to use.

Windows is a Graphical User Interface (or **GUI**, pronounced *gooey*). What this means is that you work mainly by pointing at and clicking on symbols on the screen, rather than by typing commands. It is largely intuitive – i.e. the obvious thing to do is probably the right thing, and is tolerant of mistakes. Most can be corrected as long as you tackle them straight away, and many can be corrected easily.

## The desktop

One of the ideas behind the design of Windows and of most Windows applications is that you should be able to treat the screen as you would a desk. This is where you can lay out your papers and books and tools to suit your own way of working. You may want to have more than one set of papers to hand at a time – so Windows lets you run several programs at once. You are likely to work mainly with one set of papers, with others nearby for reference – so Windows lets you make one program's window lie prominently on the top, with bits of others peeking around it, where they can easily be picked up.

Currently working on this.
Window on top.

Need to get at these often.
Windows open but tucked beneath.

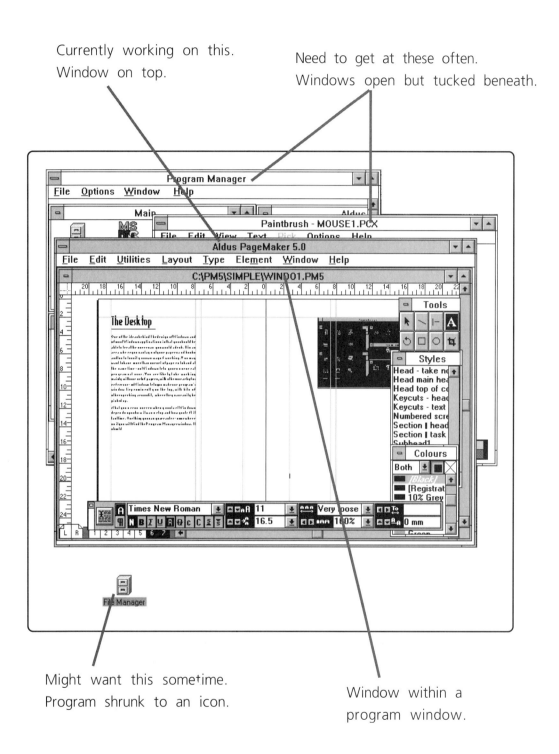

Might want this sometime.
Program shrunk to an icon.

Window within a
program window.

# The window frame

This is more than just a pretty border. It contains all the controls you need for adjusting the display.

## Frame edge

This has a control system built into it. When a window is in Restore mode – i.e. smaller than full-screen – you can drag on the edge to make it larger or smaller. (See Changing the size, page 39.)

## Title bar

This is to remind you of where you are and is used for moving the window. Drag on this and the window moves. (See Moving windows, page 38.)

## Maximize, Minimize and Restore

These buttons change the display mode. Only one of Maximize and Restore will be visible at any one time. Any window can be of fixed size, filling the whole screen, be of variable size, anywhere on screen, or be compressed into an icon. (See Changing Display Modes, page 36.)

## Control menu button

Clicking this once will open the Control menu, which offers keyboard alternatives to the Display mode buttons, plus a couple of other commands. (See Changing Display Modes, page 36.) More interesting for mouse operators, is the fact that double-clicking this button will close down the window, ending whatever program was running there.

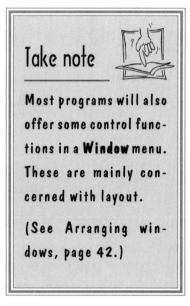

## Take note

Most programs will also offer some control functions in a **Window** menu. These are mainly concerned with layout.

(See Arranging windows, page 42.)

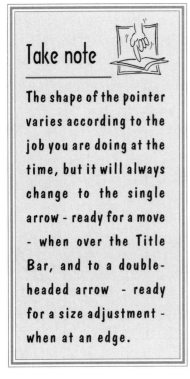

## Take note

The shape of the pointer varies according to the job you are doing at the time, but it will always change to the single arrow - ready for a move - when over the Title Bar, and to a double-headed arrow - ready for a size adjustment - when at an edge.

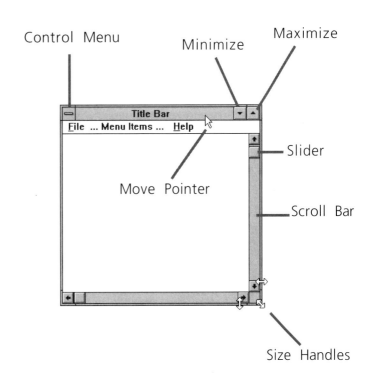

## Scroll bars

These are present on the right side and bottom of the frame if the display contained by the window is too big to fit within it. The **Sliders** in the Scroll Bars show you where your view is, relative to the overall display. Moving these allows you to view a different part of the display. (See Scrolling, page 40.)

# Taming the mouse

You can't do much in Windows until you have tamed the mouse. It is used for locating the cursor, for selecting from menus, highlighting, moving and changing the size of objects, and much more. It won't bite, but it will wriggle until you have shown it who's in charge, so get your hand round it now.

## The mouse run

To control the mouse effectively you need a good mouse-run. Clear an area about the size of this book (opened out), to the side of the keyboard. It should be lined as mice don't run well on hard desktops. You can get special mouse mats. I use a thin pad of A4 paper. Mice seem to prefer it and I've always got somewhere to jot down notes.

## The mouse and the cursor

Moving the mouse rolls the ball that it contains. The ball turns the sensor rollers and these tranmit the movement to the cursor. Straightforward? Yes, but there are a couple of points to note.

- First, if you are so close to the edge of the mouse run that you cannot move the cursor any further, pick up the mouse and plonk it back into the middle. If the ball doesn't move, the cursor doesn't move.

- Second, you can set up the mouse so that when the mouse is moved faster, the cursor moves further. (See Adjusting the mouse, page 23.) Watch out for this when working on other people's machines.

The Left button is the main one

The Right is rarely used

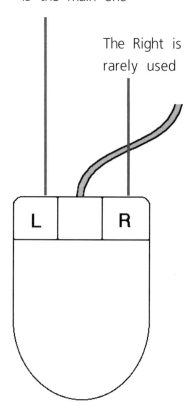

Top View - rest your palm on the rounded end and let your first two fingers lie on the right and left buttons.

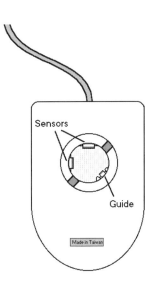

Bottom View - with the ball taken out to show the rollers.

# Mouse actions

## Click

A simple press and release. Click on menus to make a choice; click on objects to select them. Use the left button unless it specifically says **Right Click**.

## Double click

Click twice in quick succession. How quick, is something you can determine for yourself. (See Adjusting the mouse, page 23.) Keep the touch light, and listen for the little clicks.

## Hold and drag

Keep the left button down while moving the mouse. This is used for moving, resizing, drawing and similar jobs.

## Tip

A clean mouse is a happy mouse. If it starts to play up, take out the ball and clean it and the rollers with a damp tissue. Check for fluff build-up on the roller axles and remove any with tweezers.

# The keyboard

Most of the command and control operations can be handled quite happily by the mouse alone, leaving the keyboard for data entry. However, there are some operations where the keys must be used as well as the mouse, and if you prefer typing to mousing, it is possible to do most jobs - though not all - from the keyboard.

The keyboard on most desktop PCs follow the same pattern, with only minor variations. Portables are different, as they have to cram the same functions into a smaller space. If you are working on a portable, dig out its manual now and find which keys, or combination of keys, are the equivalent of those listed here.

## The alphanumeric keypad

This makes up the main body of the board. Around the central block of letter and number keys you will see control keys - usually in a different colour. There is some duplication here, with a **[Ctrl]** (Control) and [ ⇧ ](Shift) key on either side.

## The function keys

Many operations can be run from these keys, instead of the mouse - if you can be bothered to learn the keystrokes. Personally I can't. The only one really worth remembering is **[F1]**. This will always call up Help.

## Key guide

**[Esc]** - to Escape from trouble. Use it to cancel bad choices.

**[Tab]** - often used to move between objects on screen, as well as for tabs in text.

**[Caps Lock]** - only put this on when you want to type a lot of capitals. For the odd one use **[Shift]**. The Caps Lock light shows if it is on.

**[Shift]** - hold down to get capitals and the symbols on the number keys. Also used with the mouse to change its effect.

**[Ctrl]** - often used with other keys to give keystroke alternatives to mouse commands.

**[Alt]** - used, like **[Ctrl]**, in combination with other keys.

**[Backspace]** - rubs out the character to the left of the text cursor.

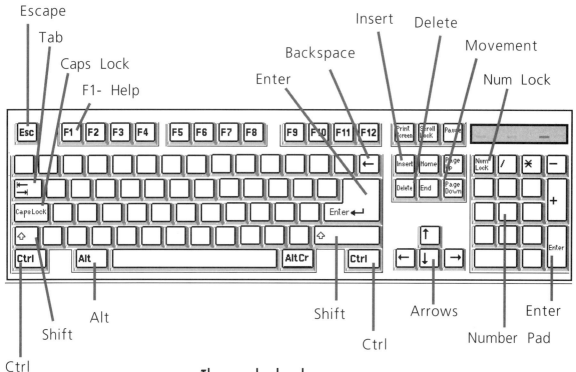

Escape
Tab
Caps Lock
F1- Help

Insert  Delete
Movement
Backspace
Num Lock
Enter

Shift  Alt  Shift  Arrows  Enter
Ctrl  Ctrl  Number Pad
Shift
Ctrl

## The control sets

These are the three small clusters to the right of the main pad. The **Arrow** keys, at the bottom, can often be used instead of the mouse for moving the cursor. Above them are more movement keys, which will let you jump around in text. **[Insert]** and **[Delete]** are also here. (See the Key Guide.) The three at the top serve special purposes, and can be ignored for now.

## The number pad

This is a dual purpose set. When the **[Num Lock]** is off, the number pad echoes the movement control keys, rather than giving numbers. Leave it on. If you are doing any calculations, it is easier to get the + - * / symbols from here than from the main keypad. Note that there is an **[Enter]** key on the Number Pad.

[Enter] (or Return) - used at the end of a line of text or to set an operation going.

[Insert] - used in typing to switch between Insert and Overtype modes.

[Delete] - rubs out the character to the right of the cursor, but will also delete files, programs and screen objects. Use with care.

# Making choices

There are many situations where you have to specify a filename or an option. Sometimes you have to type in what you want, but in most cases, it only takes a click of the mouse or a couple of keystrokes.

## Menus

To pull one down from the menu bar click on it, or press [Alt] and the underlined letter – usually the initial.

To select an item from a menu, click on it or type its underlined letter.

Some items are *toggle* switches. Selecting them turns an option on or off. A tick beside the name shows that the option is currently on.

If you select an item whose name has three dots after it, a dialog box will open to get more information from you.

## Dialog boxes

These vary, but will always have:

- an **OK** button, to click when you have set the options, selected the file or whatever;

- a **Cancel** button, in case you decide the whole thing was a mistake;

- a **Help** button, to bring up a relevant Help page.

Click or press [Alt]-[F]

Dialog box will follow

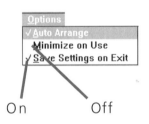

On                    Off

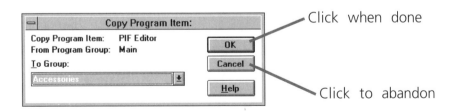

Click when done

Click to abandon

Only these two

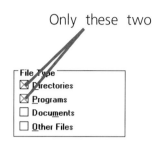

This one please

# Check boxes

These are used where there are several options, and you can use as many as you like at the same time.

A cross in the box shows that the option has been selected.

# Radio buttons

These are used for either-or options. Only one of the set can be selected.

The selected option is shown by black blob in the middle.

# Drop-down lists

If you see a slot with a down arrow button on its right, clicking the button will drop down a list.

Select from the list by clicking on your choice.

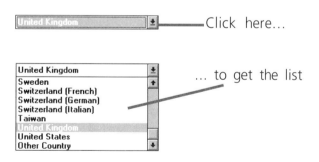

Click here...

... to get the list

# Summary

❑ Windows is an **intuitive** system – if something *feels* right, it probably *is* right.

❑ All Windows software works in much the same way, so once you have got the hang on one program, you are half way to learning the next.

❑ The **mouse** is an important tool. Keep it clean and give yourself a good mouse run.

❑ Some operations are easier with **keys**, and just a few can only be done from the keyboard.

❑ **Selections** can usually be made by picking from a list or clicking on a button or check box.

# 2 Help

# Searching for help

## Basic steps

All Windows applications manage help in the same way. The Help pages can be called up by pressing **[F1]** or selecting **Help** from the menu bar. Usually the simplest way to find the help you need is to **Search** for it.

## Search

This is organised through an cross-referenced list of terms, and is usually quicker – if you know the jargon. The window has two panes, headed **Show Topics** and **Go To**. **Show Topics** displays an alphabetical list of references; **Go To** displays the titles of the related Help pages. To find a topic, you first select its reference.

1. Select **Help** from the menu bar.

2. Choose **Search for Help on...**

3. If you are Searching, start to type the term into the slot to focus the **Show Topics** list or use the scroll bar to find the topic.

4. Select your reference from the **Show Topics** pane.

5. Select a page from the lower pane and click **Go To**.

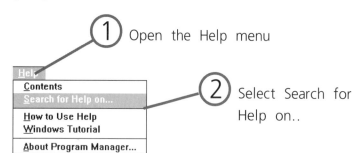

① Open the Help menu

② Select Search for Help on..

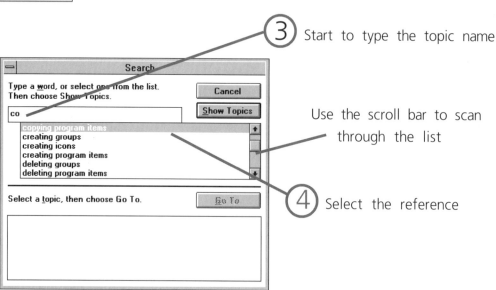

③ Start to type the topic name

Use the scroll bar to scan through the list

④ Select the reference

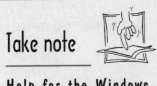
# Typing in Show Topics

Scrolling through the list will show you what is there, but you can often get to the right place faster by starting to type the key word into the top slot. The list responds instantly to your typing, so that it displays those items that start with the letters you have typed. There is no quick way to get through a Go To list, but most are fairly short – some only contain one page.

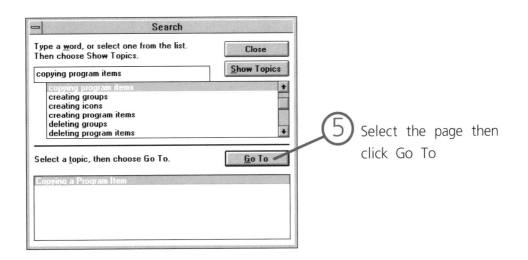

⑤ Select the page then click Go To

# Inside help

If you don't know the name that identifies what you are looking for, the best bet is to take the **Contents** appraoch, then browse round the Help pages by jumping.

## Jumps

At any point in the Help pages, if you see an icon or an underlined word (usually in green on a colour system), clicking on this will take you to its Help page.

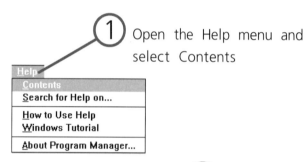

① Open the Help menu and select Contents

② See what is available

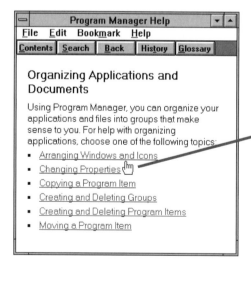

③ Point to the page title and click

1 Open the **Help** menu and choose **Contents**.

2 Read through the list of main headings to find the one that looks most promising.

3 Move the pointer to the name – the arrow should turn into a hand – and click.

4 You may find another list of topics or items underlined in the text. Point and click on any of these to jump to the related Help page.

## Looking back

Windows keeps a track of your progress through the Help pages in a history file, and offers several ways to return to an earlier topic.

**Back** will take you back one page at a time;

**History** will show you where you have been, and selecting a page from the displayed list will jump you directly back to it.

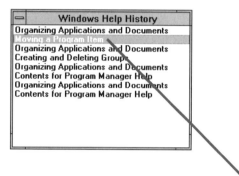

Point and click to jump back to the page

 **Tip**

Some applications have an **Always on Top** option that keeps the Help pages to hand, but can be a bit much. If you want to use this, shrink the Help window down to a reasonable size and push it into a corner, out of the way.

# Summary

❑ Help is always available. It won't necessarily solve your problems, but it is always worth a try.

❑ Use the **Search** when you can put a name to the topic that you need help with.

❑ Use the **Contents** route when you want to explore what is there.

# 3 The control panel

# The settings

Control Panel

The **Control Panel** allows you to customise many of the features of Windows to your own need and tastes.

Some settings are best left at their defaults set when Windows was first installed; some should be set when new hardware or software is added to the system; some should be set once and then left alone; a few can be fiddled with whenever you feel like a change.

Seven of the control settings are covered in this section. These are not:

386 Enhanced

**386 Enhanced** controls the use memory and processing power. Sensible defaults will have been set for this during the Windows installation. Any changes should be left until you have had more experience.

Ports

**Ports** controls the way the serial ports behave. You would only want to change these if you had a modem or serial printer connected.

Drivers

**Drivers** is used when you add new hardware to the system. A driver is a piece of software that controls the interaction between the PC and the added kit.

Sound

**Sound** allows you to add sound effects to certain events, but is only available if you have a sound card in your PC.

Printers

**Printers** is very important. Its routines can also be accessed through the Print Manager, and we will come back to them in Section 10.

Mouse

# Adjusting the mouse

1 Adjust the **Tracking Speed**.

2 Move the mouse and watch the pointer.

3 Adjust the **Double Click Speed**.

4 Double-click on the **Test** area.

5 Back to 1 until you are happy.

The **Tracking Speed** links speed and distance, so that the faster you move the mouse, the further the pointer goes. The faster the tracking speed, the more exaggerated the effect. At the Fastest setting, a short, quick flick will take the pointer across the screen where it can be accurately positioned with slow movements.

The **Double-Click Speed** determines the difference between a double click and two separate clicks.

*Don't* **Swap Left/Right Buttons** unless you are the only one who uses the system, and it is the only system that you use. You will only confuse yourself and others.

**Mouse Trails** is an option only for portables with LCD screens. It is very easy to lose sight of a moving mouse on these unless they leave trails behind them.

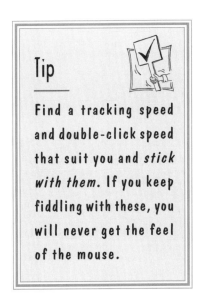

## Tip

**Find a tracking speed and double-click speed that suit you and *stick with them*. If you keep fiddling with these, you will never get the feel of the mouse.**

Needs a lot of mouse space          Very volatile

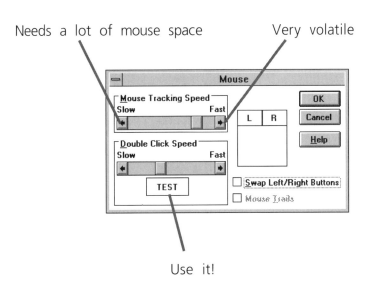

Use it!

23

# Adjusting the keys

Keyboard

This is a small but significant adjustment. When you hold down a key, the system will – after a little while – start to repeat that key's character. This can be very useful if you want a whole string of dashes or asterisks to create a line across the screen.

The two questions are, how long is a little while, and how fast should the characters be repeated?

The answers depend entirely upon your touch and your proficiency as a typist. If you are a struggling two-finger typist, go for a Long **Delay** and a Slow **Repeat Rate** or you will find that you are regularly getting more out of the keyboard than you wanted.

After you have changed a setting, click on the **Test** slot and hold down a key. Do you have easily enough time to get your finger clear before it starts to repeat, and after the system has repeated enough characters?

## Basic steps

1  Adjust the **Delay**.

2  Adjust the **Repeat Rate**.

3  Click on the **Test** area and hold down a key.

4  Back to 1 until you are happy.

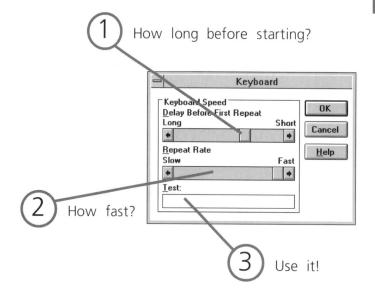

24

Color

# The color scheme

## Basic steps

1 Pick a **Color Scheme** from the list.

2 Check it out on the sample window.

3 If you want to fine-tune a schem, open the **Color Palette**.

4 Choose the **Element** you want to change.

5 Pick (or Define) a colour for it.

6 Click **OK** when all elements are as you want them.

The Windows default colour scheme is the equivalent of the magnolia paint that they use on new houses – so bland that no one is offended by it. Find one that suits your personality and the PC's surroundings. There are plenty to choose from, ranging from the garish to the sombre. Pull down the Color Schemes list and try them. The sample window will show you what colour each element will be. If you cannot find exactly what you want, make up your own.

Clicking on [ **Color Palette >>** ] opens up a second panel of the dialog box. Here you can specify the colour of each element.

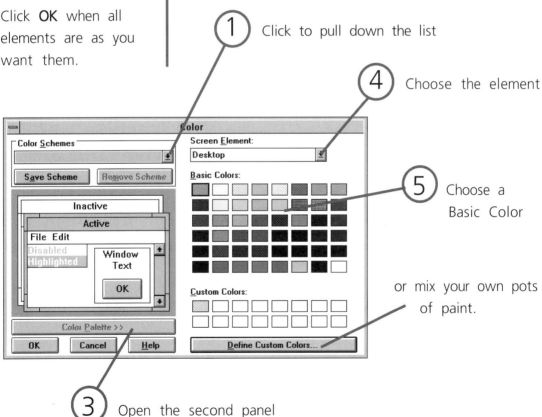

① Click to pull down the list

④ Choose the element

⑤ Choose a Basic Color

or mix your own pots of paint.

③ Open the second panel

# Designing the desktop

This may seem to be pure frills and fancies, but it does have a serious purpose. You could well be spending a lot of time in front of your screen. Having one that you can see clearly and use comfortably can make a significant difference to your efficiency.

The **Pattern** is the one behind the names of icons at the bottom of the screen. Leave this at None, unless you want to make them almost unreadable.

**Screen Saver**s are a good idea. If a static image is left on too long, it can burn into the screen. The screen savers will either blank the screen or switch to a moving image after the system has been left inactive for a few minutes. **Test** the ones that are on offer. **Setup** allows you to adjust the images.

There is a small industry churning out weird and wonderful screen savers for you to buy, if you want something different.

The **Setup** dialog box for the Marquee screen saver is shown here.

Tip

Make sure **Fast "Alt+Tab" Switching** is turned on. This is the feature that lets you cycle between open applications by holding **[Alt]** and pressing **[Tab]**. (See page 34.)

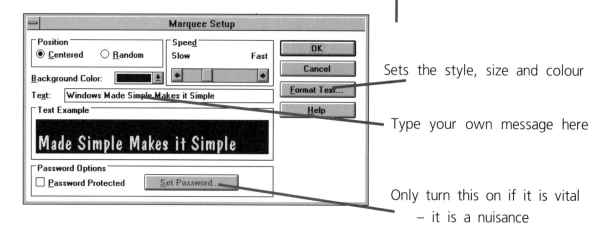

Sets the style, size and colour

Type your own message here

Only turn this on if it is vital – it is a nuisance

26

The **Wallpaper** is the background to the desktop. Some are hideous, but others are acceptable. If you run your windows with much wallpaper showing, aim for something unobtrusive.

The supplied patterns can be edited with Paintbrush, if you feel artistic, or you can use any bitmapped graphic instead of one of them. With a large image, set it in the **Centre** rather than duplicate it as a **Tile**.

In the **Icons** section, make sure that **Wrap Title** is turned on. This makes long names spread over two lines, rather than running into their neighbours.

You may want to adjust the **Cursor Blink Rate** to one that sits easy on your eyes.

Leave the rest at their default settings – they are fine.

Click to drop down the options list

Make sure this is on

Adjust with the arrows or type in a number

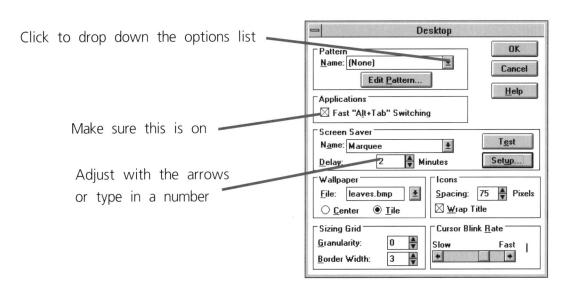

# International settings

These control the keyboard layout, units of measurement and the formats used by all Windows applications in displaying dates, time, currency and other numbers.

When you first installed Windows, you should have been asked for the **Country** and **Language** settings, and these determine the defaults for the rest. By and large they should be right, though you may want to adjust some.

The [ Change... ] buttons open dialog boxes for fine tuning the formats. This is mainly a matter of selecting from option lists. The **Date** box is a good example.

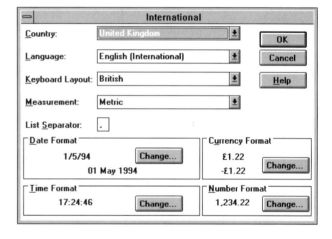

Windows has two Date formats.

● Short consists of numbers only.

● Long uses the month name, and can include the day name.

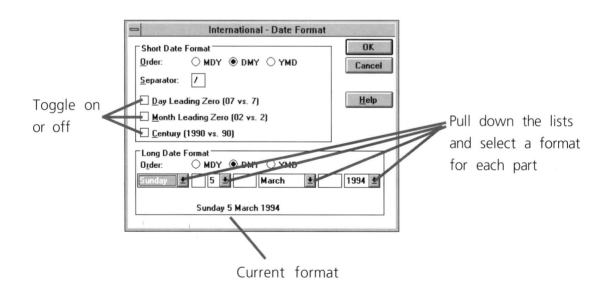

Toggle on or off

Pull down the lists and select a format for each part

Current format

# Basic steps

Date/Time

# Date and time

❏ To set the clock

1 Move the highlight from one element of the **Date** and **Time** to the next with **[Tab]** or the mouse.

2 Change the setting with the ⬍ arrows or by typing a new value.

3 Click **OK** when the clock is correct.

❏ To see the Clock

1 Run the 🕐 **Clock** program, from the Accessories group.

2 Adjust its display with the options in its **Settings** menu.

PCs have an internal clock/calendar that is kept ticking by a fixed rechargeable battery. Once it has been set correctly, it should rarely need altering. (Especially if, like me, you run on GMT throughout the year.) Some people find that their clocks lose slightly, and this is seems to be caused by certain poorly designed programs that interfere with the regular updating of the clock.

If you do find that your clock keeps *very* poor time, it is probably a failing battery, and replacing that is a job for an expert.

If you want to keep an eye the time, run the Clock program in a little window. Personally, I prefer a watch and a clearer screen.

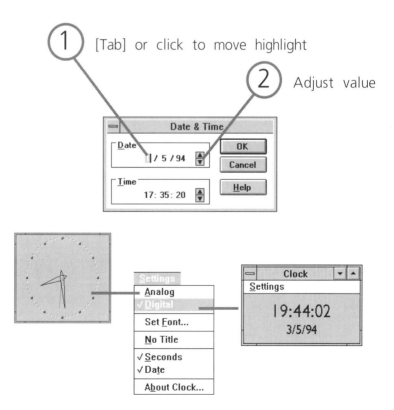

① [Tab] or click to move highlight

② Adjust value

# Tip

If you select **No title** on the **Clock**, double click anywhere on the dial when you want to get the title bar back.

29

# Fonts

There is one school of thought that says you can never have enough fonts. There is a decent core supplied with Windows itself, and you will normally acquire more with any word-processor and desktop publishing packages that you install. If these are not enough for you, there are whole disks full of fonts available commercially and through the shareware distributors. Check the adverts in any PC magazine if you are interested.

Installing new fonts is quick and easy. Removing unwanted ones is equally easy and worth doing. You will save space on the hard disk and have a shorter set to hunt through when you are setting a font in an application.

The **Fonts** dialog box has a **Sample** panel which shows the appearance of the selected font.

## Basic steps

1 Place the disk of new fonts into a drive.

2 Click the **Add** button.

3 At the dialog box, select the drive, and directory.

4 Wait while the system reads the names of the fonts on the disk.

5 Click **Select All**, or work through the list and select the ones you want to install.

6 Click **OK**

7 Back at the **Fonts** dialog box, check the Sample display for each new font and select and **Remove** any you don't want.

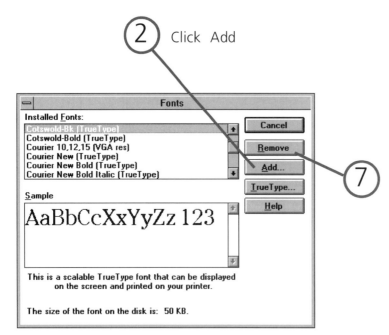

② Click Add

⑦ Remove unwanted ones

**30**

# True Type

A True Type font looks (almost) exactly the same on screen as it will when printed – at least it will do if you have turned the **Enable** option on. Those that are not True Type are represented on screen by the nearest Windows equivalent.

In the True Type dialog box, check that **Enable** is turned *on*, and **Show Only True Type** *off*.

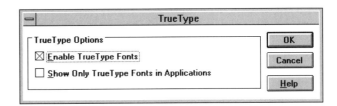

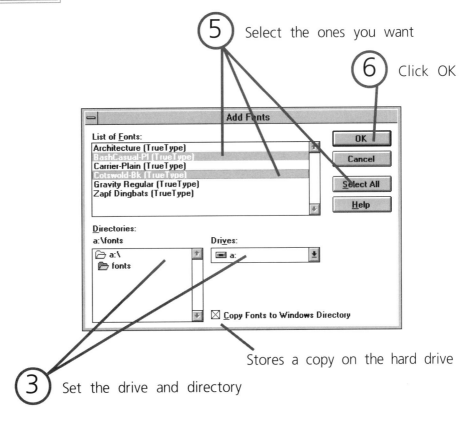

⑤ Select the ones you want

⑥ Click OK

Stores a copy on the hard drive

③ Set the drive and directory

# Summary

- ❑ The **Control Panel** contains a group of routines that determine the settings of some of the most basic features of how Windows works.

- ❑ Adjust the **Mouse** and **Keyboard** responses to your own needs at an early stage, then leave them alone.

- ❑ There are plenty of alternative **Color Schemes**, and each element of the screen can be displayed in your own choice of colour.

- ❑ You have a choice of **Wallpapers** for your **Desktop**, or you can use any picture as a backdrop.

- ❑ **Screen Savers** really do help to save the screen – and they could carry an advert for you when you are not working!

- ❑ The **International** settings control the appearance of dates, times, numbers and currency in all Windows applications.

- ❑ **Date** and **Time** should only need setting once – and adjusting at the start and end of Summer Time.

- ❑ Extra **Fonts** can be added to Windows, but be selective, or be prepared to spend ages hunting through extensive lists every time you want one.

# 4 Window Control

# Moving between windows

You can only do things in, or to, one window at a time, and this is the active window - marked by a highlighted title bar. (If the window has been reduced to an icon, it is 'active' if its name is highlighted.) So, before you can do much else, you should find out how to move the focus from one window to another.

As long as you can see the window you want, making it active is simply a matter of clicking on it. You can click anywhere, though the title bar or the main working are the safest places. There are so many controls in the frame that clicking on this can have unexpected results.

If you cannot see the window, use [Alt]-[Tab] to cycle through the open windows to get to the one you want.

## Basic steps

1 Hold **[Alt]** and press **[Tab]**. The name of an open window appears on the screen.

2 If this is not one you want, press **[Tab]** until it appears.

3 Release **[Alt]** and the named window will come to the front.

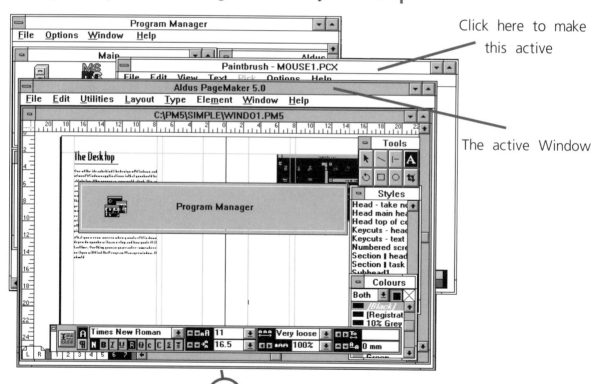

Click here to make this active

The active Window

③ Release **[Alt]** when you see the one you want

# Basic steps

# The Task List

1 Press [Ctrl]-[Esc] to open the **Task List**.

2 Use the mouse or the Up/Down arrow keys to select a program

3 **Switch To** it, or

4 close it down with **End Task**.

When your windows have got into a mess – as well they can – and you cannot see the one you want, use the Task List It displays a list of the programs that you are running at the time, and offers a set of options. Use **Switch To**, to make a window active.

If you just want to tidy up your screen, use the **Cascade**, **Tile** or **Arrange Icons** options. (See Arranging Windows, page 42)

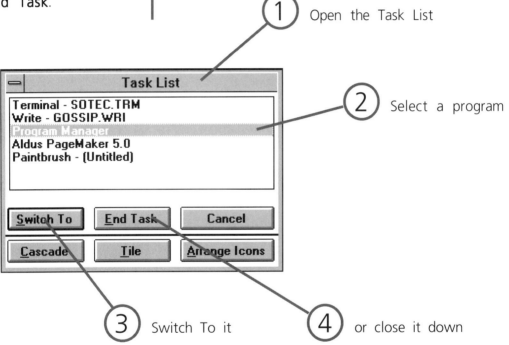

① Open the Task List

② Select a program

③ Switch To it

④ or close it down

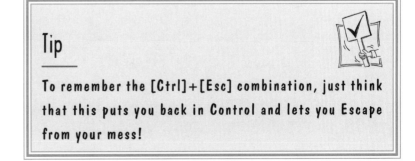

## Tip

To remember the [Ctrl]+[Esc] combination, just think that this puts you back in Control and lets you Escape from your mess!

# Changing display modes

Clicking on the buttons in the top right corner of the frame is the simplest way to switch between **Maximize** and **Restore** modes, and to **Minimize** a window. If you prefer it can be done by clicking the top left button and using the options on the Control Menu.

| Restore | |
|---|---|
| <u>M</u>ove | |
| <u>S</u>ize | |
| Mi<u>n</u>imize | |
| Ma<u>x</u>imize | |
| <u>C</u>lose | Alt+F4 |
| S<u>w</u>itch To... | Ctrl+Esc |

## The Control menu

One or more options will be 'greyed out' to show that they don't apply at the time. This menu came from a variable size window. One from a full-screen window would have **Move**, **Size** and **Maximize** in grey.

**Close** shuts down the window. If you close Program Manager, it shuts down Windows.

The **Switch To** option opens the Task List (see previous page.)

- ❏ **To make a window full-screen**

  Click ▲ or select **Maximize** from the Control Menu

- ❏ **To restore a window to variable size**

  Click ⬍ or select **Restore** from the Control Menu

- ❏ **To shrink a window to an icon**

  Click ▼ or select **Minimize** from the Control Menu

## Tip

If you are only working in one window, Maximize it. This gives you the largest working area and avoids any confusion with any other windows that are lying around and behind it.

# Restoring an icon

Either:

**1** Double-click on the Icon, or click once and select **Restore** from its Control Menu.

or

**1** Use **[Alt]-[Tab]** to cycle through the names of the current set of windows and icons until you reach the one you want.

**2** When you release **[Alt]**, the icon is made active, and is automatically restored to a window.

If you can see the icon, you can click on it and restore it – but it may have disappeared behind another window . In this case, you can shrink the top windows to make your icon visible again, or use the **[Alt]** and **[Tab]** technique.

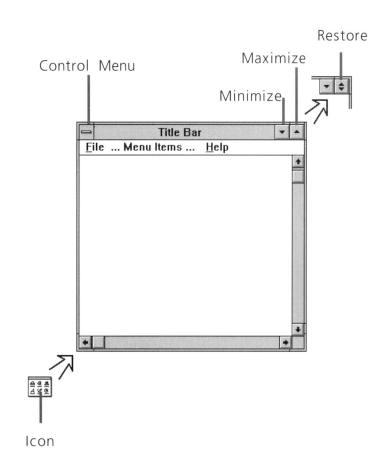

Restore

Maximize

Control Menu

Minimize

Icon

# Moving windows

When a window is in **Restore** mode – open but not full screen – it can be moved anywhere on the screen.

● If you are not careful it can be moved almost off the screen! Fortunately, at least a bit of the title bar will still be visible, and that is the handle you need to grab to pull it back into view.

1 If the Title Bar isn't highlighted, click on the window to make it the active one.

2 Point at the Title Bar and hold the left button down.

3 Drag the window to its new position - you will only see a grey outline moving.

4 Release the button.

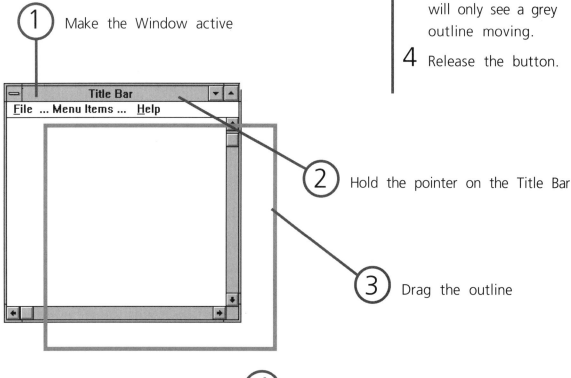

① Make the Window active

Title Bar

File ... Menu Items ... Help

② Hold the pointer on the Title Bar

③ Drag the outline

④ Release to drop into its new position

38

## Basic steps

**1** Move the pointer to the edge or corner that you want to pull in or out.

**2** When you see the double-headed arrow, hold down the mouse button.

**3** Drag the outline to the required size

**4** Release the button.

When a window is in Restore mode, you can change its size and shape by dragging the edges of the frame to new positions.

Combined with the moving facility, this lets you arrange your desktop exactly the way you like it.

● The size handles only appear when the pointer is just on an edge, and they disapear again if you go too far. Practice! You'll soon get the knack of catching them.

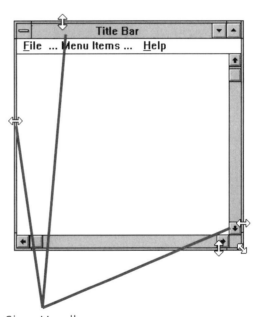

Size Handles

## Tip

The quickest way your get a window the right size, in the right place, is to use the bottom right size handle to set the shape, then drag the window into position.

# Scrolling

What you can see in a window is often only part of the story. The working area of the application may well be much larger. If there are scroll bars on the side and/or bottom of the window, this tells you that there is more material outside the frame. The scroll bars let you pull some of this material into view.

## Tip

If a window is blank — and you think there should be something there — push the sliders to the very top and left. That's where your work is likely to be.

Sliders

# Basic Scrolls

☐ Drag the **Slider** ▢ to scroll the view in the window. Keep your pointer moving straight along the bar or it won't work!

☐ Click an **Arrow** ▷ to move the slider a little way towards the arrow. Hold down for a slow continuous scroll.

☐ Click on the **Bar** above, below or beside the Slider to make it jump towards the pointer.

Write - WINARR.WRI

File  Edit  Find  Character  Paragraph  Document  Help

## Arranging Windows

Busy desktops tend to get untidy. How much disorder you can cope with, depends on you, but there comes a point for all of us when we just have to tidy up so that we can see what we are doing. There are Windows tools that will do it for you, or you can do it yourself.

Page 1

Look on the Program Manager menu bar and you will see Window. Pull this menu down and it will display the options Cascade and Tile, amongst others.These same options are on the Control menu and on the Window menu of most applications programs.

**Cascade** and **Tile** both have their limitations, but can be the basis of a well-arranged desktop. ¤

Arrow buttons

Working area

40

## Basic Steps

Either:

1 Open the program's **File** menu

2 Select **Exit**

or

1 Double-click the

**Control menu** button

3 If you have forgotten to save your work, take the opportunity that is offered to you.

When you close a window, you close down the program that was running inside it. When you close the Program Manager window, this ends your Windows session, because Program Manager is what makes Windows work.

If you haven't saved your work, most programs will point this out and give you a chance to save before closing.

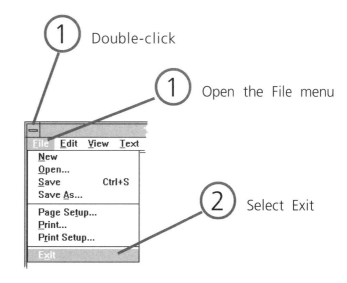

① Double-click

① Open the File menu

② Select Exit

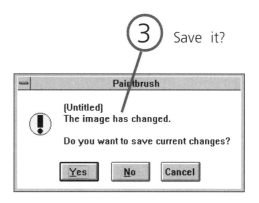

③ Save it?

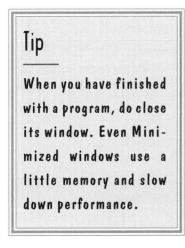

## Tip

**When you have finished with a program, do close its window. Even Minimized windows use a little memory and slow down performance.**

# Arranging windows

Busy desktops tend to get untidy. How much disorder you can cope with, depends on you, but there comes a point for all of us when we just have to tidy up so that we can see what we are doing. There are Windows tools that will do it for you, or you can do it yourself.

The Task List lets you arrange your open windows on the desktop. Open it and you will see its **Cascade** and **Tile** buttons. These same options are on the Control menu and on the Window menu of most applications programs, though they only affect the layout of windows *within* the programs.

Cascade and Tile both have their limitations, but can be the basis of a well-arranged desktop.

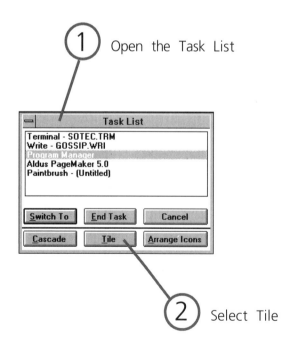

① Open the Task List

② Select Tile

1 Press **[Ctrl]-[Esc]** to open the **Task List**

2 Select **Tile**

3 **Close** any windows that are no longer wanted – do not close Program Manager!

4 **Minimize** those that you are not actively using.

5 Open the Task List and select **Tile** again to tidy up the remaining windows.

6 If you only want to work in one window at a time, **Maximize** it, and **Restore** it back into the arrangement when you have done.

7 If you need to have ready access to two or more, move and size themto adjust the balance of the layout.

# Tile

Tile arranges open windows side by side, in one or two rows. The windows are all small, but it works for things like Program Manager, as the little windows are still large enough to display half a dozen or so icons. It is not really suitable for windows that you want to do any serious work in.

The active window

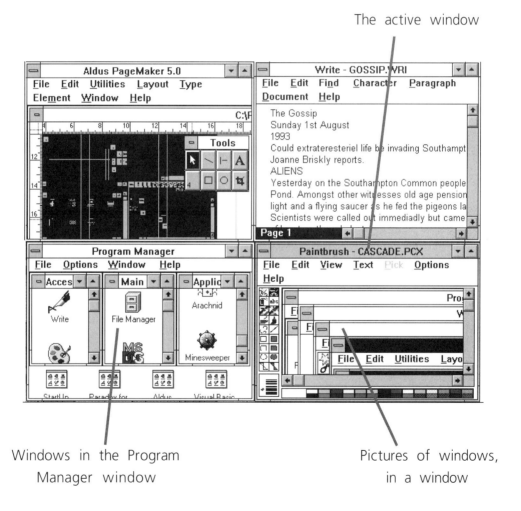

Windows in the Program Manager window

Pictures of windows, in a window

# Cascade

Cascade arranges all open windows as overlapping sheets. The current one will be at the front, and the others tucked behind with only their title bars showing. Click on the bar, or any other visible part of a lower window, to bring it to the top - at the same position.

The Cascade arrangement has the advantage of making all windows visible, while keeping the current one prominent. It is not suitable if you want access to two or more windows at once, so that you can refer to other data or copy items from one to another.

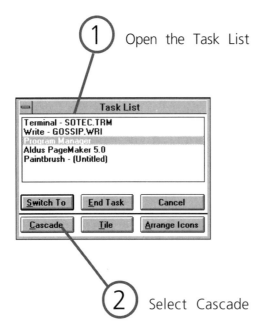

Open the Task List

Select Cascade

1 Press [Ctrl]-[Esc] to open the **Task List**

2 Select **Cascade**. Your working window should be on top.

3 **Close** any unwanted windows

4 Press [Ctrl]-[Esc] to reopen the **Task List** and **Cascade** to tidy up the display.

5 When you want to move to a new window, click on its title bar.

## Tip

**Arrange Icons is rarely worth bothering with unless you have an awful lot of them scattered around.**

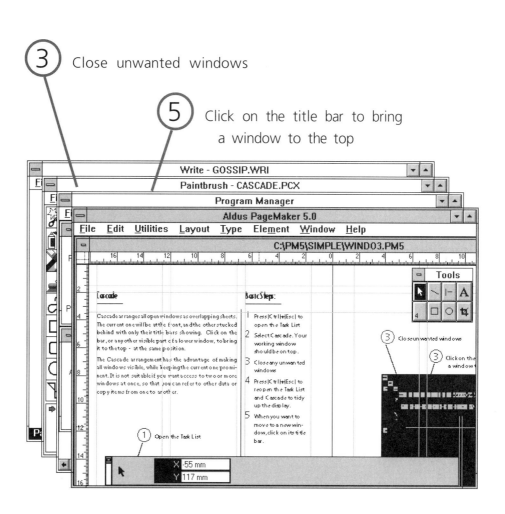

3 Close unwanted windows

5 Click on the title bar to bring a window to the top

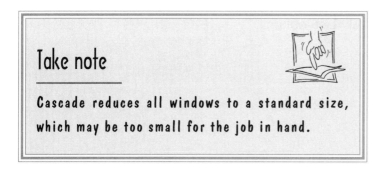

## Take note

Cascade reduces all windows to a standard size, which may be too small for the job in hand.

# Summary

❑ You can move between windows by clicking on any visible part of them – though the active parts of the frame should be avoided.

❑ Pressing [Ctrl]-[Esc] brings up the **Task List** which can help you to see what you are doing.

❑ Windows can be displayed in **Maximize** (full-screen) or **Restore** (variable size) modes, or **Minimized** to icons.

❑ **Icons** can be restored to full size by clicking on them.

❑ Pressing [Alt]-[Tab] will let you cycle through the open windows until you get to the one you want.

❑ A window can be **moved** about the screen by dragging on its title bar.

❑ You can change the **size** by dragging on any of its edges.

❑ The **scroll bars** will let you move the working area inside a window.

❑ **Closing** a window closes its program.

❑ Windows can be arranged on the desktop by picking **Cascade** or **TIle** from the **Task List** options.

# 5 Program Manager

# What is it?

Program Manager is what makes Windows tick. How it works is irrelevant to most of us. The important thing is what you see and how you use it.

## Icons

The Program Manager window displays icons, that represent the programs that you can run under Windows. These are only representations, and if you delete an icon – by mistake or intentionally – you do not delete its linked program, and the link can be easily remade.

● Clicking an icon selects it, and it can then be run, moved, or deleted.

● Double-clicking on an icon runs its program.

## Groups

The icons organised into Groups. Each group of icons has its own window, which can be Minimized out of the way, or Maximized to fill the Program Manager window. Some people like to keep their groups as icons, restoring a group only when they need to get at a program inside it. Others prefer to leave their groups windows open, so that a range of program icons are visible all the time.

The membership of the groups is not fixed. You can add or delete items, or move them into other groups. The position of the icon within the group window can also be changed. This is *your* Program Manager, and you can organise it how you like.

The initial Groups are outlined here. As soon as you start to install software on your system, you will have more groups of your own.

## The groups

❑ **Main** – programs for organising and controlling the system.

❑ **Accessories** – a simple word-processor, an art program, a calculator, a database, and a diary, amongst other useful tools. Some of these you will not want because you have bought applications that do the same jobs, only better.

❑ **Applications** contains those applications that the Setup program found when you first installed Windows.

❑ **Games** has Minesweeper – excellent for practicing your mouse skills – and a patience.

❑ **Startup** is empty – put into here any program you want to run automatically when the system starts.

# The selected icon

□ **To select an icon**
click once on it.

□ **To run a program,**
either

double-click its icon,
or

press **[Enter]** if the
icon is selected.

If an icon is highlighted – i.e. its name is shown on a coloured background – then it is selected. If it is selected, then things can happen to it. You can run its program, move it, or delete it.

Program Manager remembers the last icon selected in each group, and makes it the current selection next time that group is made active. Try it. Click on a group title bar and you will see that one of its icons is already highlighted.

Program Manager's menu bar

Group window

Selected Program icon

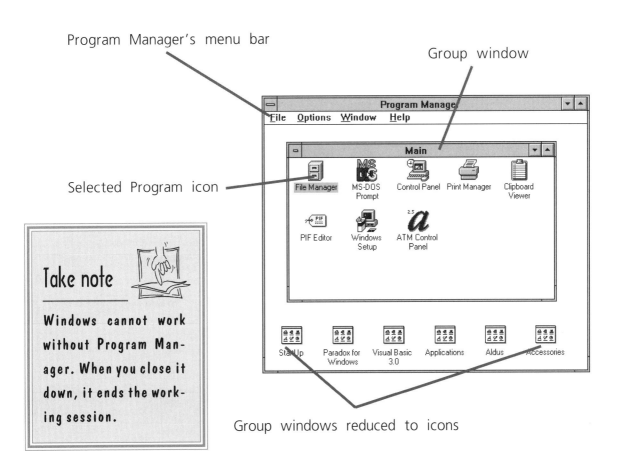

**Take note**

Windows cannot work without Program Manager. When you close it down, it ends the working session.

Group windows reduced to icons

# Arranging the display

There are three aspects to this:

- the size and shape of the Program Manager window
- the layout, size and shape of the group windows
- the position of program icons within each window

I find that the Program Manager window is best in Restore mode – filling most of the screen, but leaving a clear space at the bottom for the icons of Minimized programs.

**Group windows** can be moved and resized 'by hand', just like any other window, but the quickest way to get a tidy layout is to use the Cascade or Tile options.

❑ **Arranging groups**

1 **Restore** the windows that you want to keep open and visible.

2 **Minimize** windows that you rarely use.

3 Open the **Window** menu.

4 Select either **Cascade** or **Tile.**

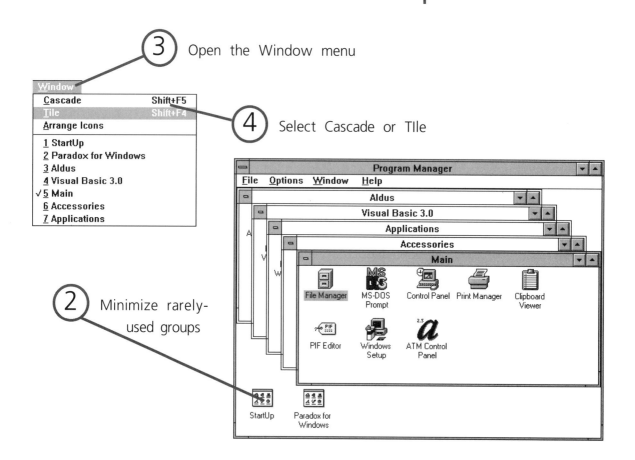

③ Open the Window menu

④ Select Cascade or TIle

② Minimize rarely-used groups

# Basic steps

❑ Arranging icons

1 Open the **Options** menu

2 If **Auto Arrange** is not checked, click on it now to turn it on.

3 **Maximize** the group window so that you can see all the icons.

4 **Drag** the most commonly used icons to the top left.

5 **Restore** the window back to its proper size.

The **icons** for the programs that you use most often, should be moved to the top left of their windows, so that they are still visible in small windows.

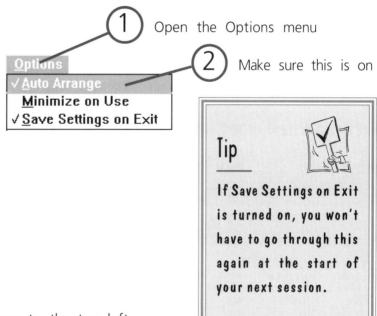

① Open the Options menu

② Make sure this is on

**Tip**

If Save Settings on Exit is turned on, you won't have to go through this again at the start of your next session.

④ Drag much-used icons to the top left

**Tip**

With the Tile layout, a range of programs is always at hand.

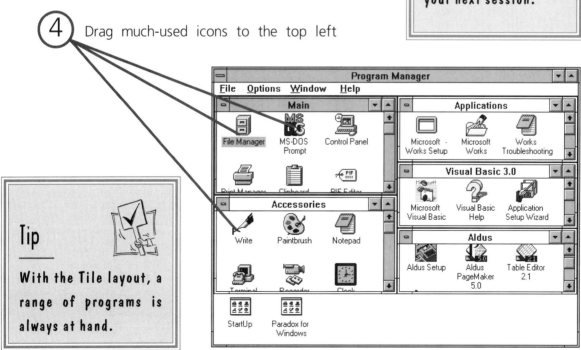

# Organising groups

If the standard icon/group organisation doesn't suit, change it. If your Applications group contains a mixed lot of programs that would be better split up into two or three groups, then make new groups and move the programs into them. If you delete the games and the unwanted accessories (after reading Slimming Windows, page 142), then you could remove both groups, pushing any remaining accessories into Main or Applications.

## Creating a new group

Once you have decided how you want to organise your icons, creating new groups is quick and easy.

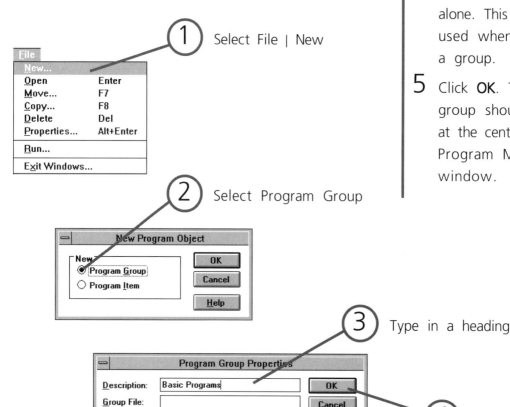

① Select File | New

② Select Program Group

③ Type in a heading

④ Click OK

## Basic steps

1 Select **New** from the **File** menu

2 In the **New Program Object** dialog box, select **Program Group** and click **OK**.

3 For the **Description**, type the heading that you want to appear in the group's title bar.

4 Leave the **Group File** alone. This is only used when renaming a group.

5 Click **OK**. The new group should appear at the centre of the Program Manager window.

## Basic steps

1 Make sure both the source and the target groups are visible – at least in part.

2 Click on the group that contains the icon, to make it active, then click on the icon.

3 Drag the icon until it is within the frame of the target group window, then release. That's it.

## Take note

**Deleting an icon does not delete its program files.**

## Adding icons to groups

● If the program you want has not yet been linked to an icon, follow the steps for creating a new icon.

● To move an existing icon into your new group, just drag it across from its old one.

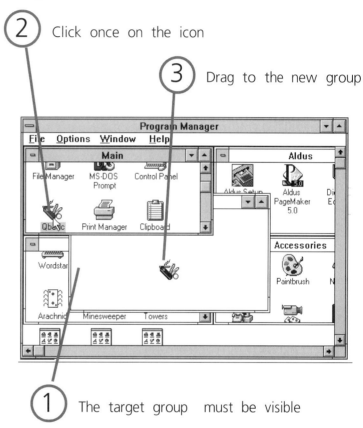

② Click once on the icon

③ Drag to the new group

① The target group must be visible

## Deleting icons and groups

● To delete an icon, select it and press [**Delete**].

● To delete a group, first delete all its icons or move them to other groups, then press [**Delete**].

In both cases, you will be prompted to confirm the deletion.

# Adding a new item

Adding an item is mainly a matter of creating an icon to make an existing program work under Windows. It is not the same as installing a new piece of software, which also involves setting up directories and copying files in from floppy disk. (See Installing programs, page 94)

There are a lot of steps, but it only takes a couple of minutes to run through them. Before you start, decide which group you want to place the icon in, and whether you need a special directory to store any data files that will be used with the program.

1 Click on the group where you want the item to go.

2 Open the **File** menu and select **New.**

3 In the **New Program Object** dialog box, click **OK** to open the **Program Item Properties** dialog box.

4 Type in a **Description** – this will be displayed beneath the icon.

5 For the **Command** line, select **Browse**.

6 In its dialog box, move to the **Drive** and **Directory** that holds the program.

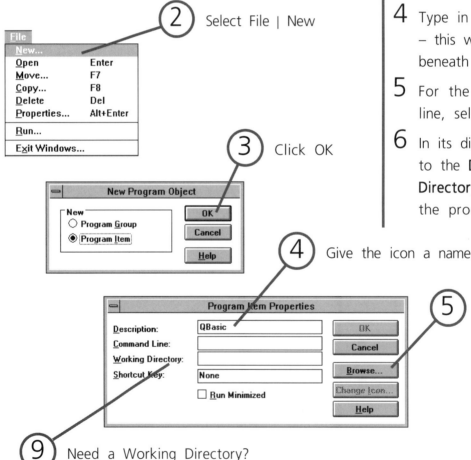

Select File | New

File
New...
Open        Enter
Move...      F7
Copy...      F8
Delete       Del
Properties...  Alt+Enter
Run...
Exit Windows...

Click OK

New Program Object
New
○ Program Group
◉ Program Item
OK
Cancel
Help

Give the icon a name

Program Item Properties
Description:        QBasic
Command Line:
Working Directory:
Shortcut Key:       None
☐ Run Minimized
OK
Cancel
Browse...
Change Icon...
Help

Select Browse

Need a Working Directory?

**7** Select the program from the **File List.**

**8** Click **OK.**

**9** Back at the **Properties** dialog box, type in a path for the **Working DIrectory**, if you want data files to be stored in a particular place.

**10** Select **Change Icon**. If the program does not have its own icon, choose one from the Program Manager set.

**11** Scroll through the display to find one the that is most apt and click OK to select it. (I'm still trying to find a use for the Swiss army knife!)

**12** Click **OK.**

**6** Set the drive and directory

**8** Click OK

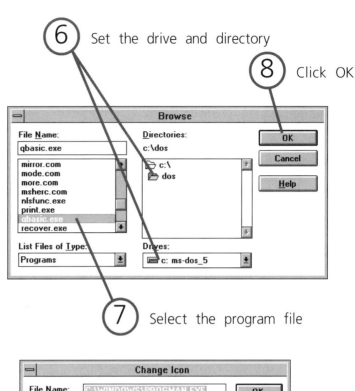

**7** Select the program file

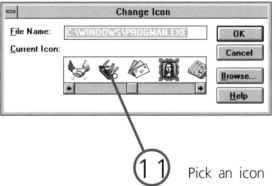

**11** Pick an icon

# Take note

When you add a **DOS** program as an item, **Windows** creates a **PIF** file (program information file) for it. This may need adjusting before the program will work properly. See Editing a PIF, page121.)

# Summary

❑ **Program Manager** is what makes Windows tick. When you close it down, you end your session.

❑ **Double-clicking** an icon runs its program

❑ **A single click** on an icon selects it. It can then be moved or deleted, or run its program.

❑ How you arrange your icons and groups is up to you.

❑ The **Window | Tile** and **Cascade** options will arrange your groups for you.

❑ New icons can be **added** at any time, as long as the program files are already on the hard disk.

❑ Icons can be **moved** from one group to another.

❑ **Deleting** an icon does not delete its program.

❑ **Unwanted groups** can be deleted, once they have been emptied of their icons.

# 6  File Manager

# Files and directories

File Manager

## What is it?

After Program Manager, File Manager is the most important part of the Windows system. This is the tool that you use to organise storage on your hard and floppy disks. With this, files and directories can be copied, moved, renamed and deleted. There is a lot to File Manager, and we will take it in four parts. In this section, we will look at the filing system, the File Manager screen display, and working with directories. In later sections, we will cover disks, different views and managing files.

## Directories

The hard disks supplied on modern PCs are typically 80 to 170 Megabytes. A Megabyte is 1 million bytes and each byte can hold one character (or part of a number or graphic ). That means that a typical hard disk can hold up to 20 million words – enough for 100 hefty novels! More to the point, if you were using it to store letters and reports, it could hold many thousands of files. It must be organised if you are ever to find your files.

Directories provide this organisation. They are containers in which related files can be placed to keep them together, and away from other files. A directory can also contain sub-directories – which can themselves by subdivided. You can think of the first level of directories as being sets of filing cabinets; the second level are drawers within the cabinets, and the next level folders within the drawers. (And the folders could have sub-dividers – there is no limit to this.)

## The jargon

- ❏ **Root** – the directory of the disk. All other directories branch off from the root.

- ❏ **Parent** – a directory that contains another.

- ❏ **Child** – a sub-directory of a Parent.

- ❏ **Branch** - the structure of sub-directories open off from a directory.

**Tip**

When planning your directory structure, aim for simplicity. Too many levels of sub-directories can make it hard to find files.

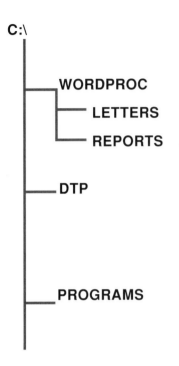

# Paths

A directory's position in the tree is described by its **path**. For most operations, you can identify a directory by clicking on it in a tree diagram, but now and then you will have to type its path. This should start at the drive letter and the root, and include every directory along the branch, with a backslash (\) between the names.

For example:

**C:\DTP**

**C:\WORDPROC\LETTERS**

When you want to know a path, look it up in the File Manager display and trace the branch down and right from the root.

## Filenames

A filename has two parts – the name and an extension.

The **name** can be up to 8 characters long and be made up of any combination of letters, digits, the under_score and a few other symbols. It cannot include spaces or punctuation. The most important thing to remember when giving a filename is that it must mean something to you, so that you can find it easily next time you come back to the job.

The **extension** can be from 0 to 3 characters, and is separated from the rest of the name by a dot. It is used to identify the nature of the file. Windows and MSDOS use the extensions COM, EXE, SYS, INI, DLL to identify special files of their own. Most applications also use their own special extensions. Word-processor files are often marked with DOC or TXT; spreadsheet files are usually WQ1 or WK1; databases files typically have DB extensions.

If you are saving a file in a word-processor, spreadsheet or other application, and are asked for a filename, you normally only have to give the first part. The application will take care of the extension. If you do need to give an extension, make it meaningful. BAK is a good extension for backup files; TXT for text files.

If File Manager asks you for a filename – and the file is in the *current* directory – type in the name and extension only. If the file is in *another* directory, type in the path, followed by the filename, with a backslash separator.

For example:

**MYFILE.DOC**

**C:\WORPROC\REPORTS\MAY25.TXT**

**A:\MYFILE.BAK**

# The file icons

**The display**

- 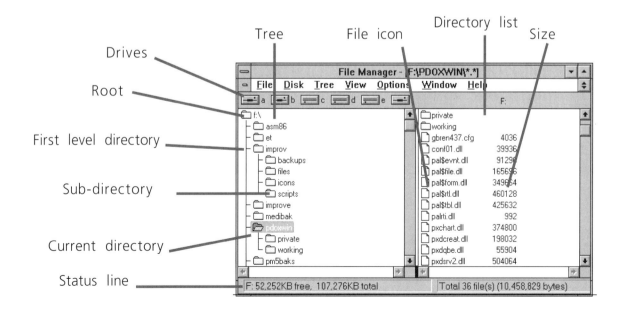 The current (open) directory

- ▢ A directory

- ▭ A program file

- ▤ A data file associated with a program

- ▯ An ordinary data file

- ▯ A 'hidden' file

File Manager window has the usual frame controls and menu bar. Beneath this is a set of icons representing the hard and floppy **drives** on the system.

The main working area can contain several windows at once. Each window is split, with the structure, or *Tree*, on the left, and the file list, or *Directory*, on the right.

The **Tree** may show the first level of directories only, but can be expanded to show some or all of the subdirectories. (See Trees and branches, oveleaf.)

The **Directory** shows the files and sub-directories in the currently selected directory. Each filename is accompanied by a small icon which indicates its nature. Additional details about the file can also be shown if required. (See Directory information, page 76.)

The **Status line** shows the number and total size of the files in the directory, on the right, and either the space on the whole disk, or the size of the selected files, on the left.

# Trees and branches

The tree can be shown in outline form, or with some or all of its branches shown in full. The level of expansion can be controlled with the options on the **Tree** menu, and – as usual – with mouse clicks.

The best display is always the simplest that will show you all you need. In most cases, this means most of the tree is collapsed back to its first level of main directories, with one or two branches expanded to show particular sub-directories. Now and then it is worth expanding the whole tree, just to get an idea of the overall structure and to see how sub-directories fit together.

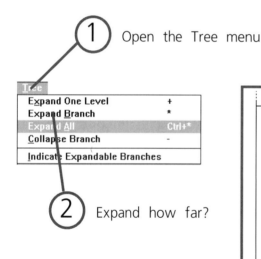

Open the Tree menu

Expand how far?

The whole tree can be over-whelming – this is just a small part of a fairly typical C:\ drive

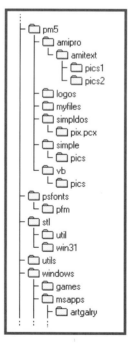

❏ **To expand a branch by one level:**

either

1   Select the directory.

2   Open the **Tree** menu

3   Select **Expand One Level**

or

1   Double-click on the directory icon

❏ **To expand a branch fully:**

either

1   Select the directory

2   Open the **Tree** menu

3   Select **Expand Branch**

or

1   Double-click on the main directory icon

2   When the next level of is shown, double-click on each icon, repeating for all levels.

❏ **To expand the whole tree:**

1   Open the **Tree** menu

2   Select **Expand All**

# Basic steps

1 Open the **Tree** menu

2 Select **Indicate Expandable Branches** to toggle the marking on and off.

To find out which directories have networks of branches, use the **Indicate Expandable Branches** option. This marks the directory icons with symbols:

⊞ has branches, and can be expanded

▭ no branching sub-directories

⊟ has branches and they are already visible.

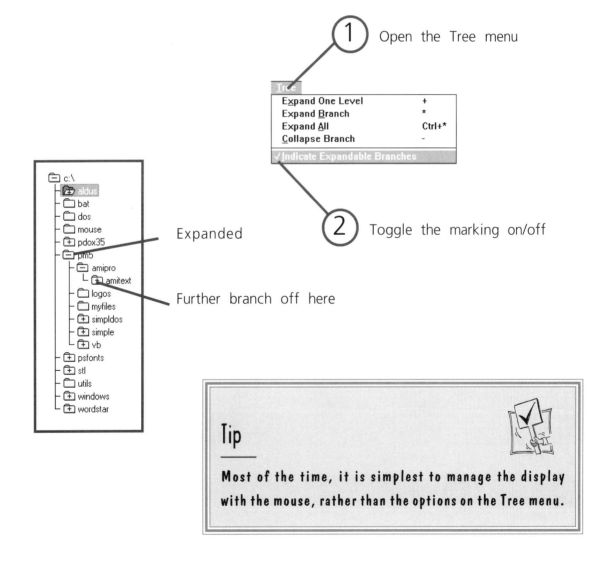

① Open the Tree menu

| Tree | |
|---|---|
| **E**xpand One Level | + |
| Expand **B**ranch | * |
| Expand **A**ll | Ctrl+* |
| **C**ollapse Branch | - |
| ✓ Indicate Expandable Branches | |

Expanded

② Toggle the marking on/off

Further branch off here

## Tip

**Most of the time, it is simplest to manage the display with the mouse, rather than the options on the Tree menu.**

# Creating a directory

Organised people set up their directories before they need them, so that they have places to store their letters – private and business, reports – for each department, memos, notes, and whatever, when they start to write them on their new system. They have a clear idea of the tree structure that they want, and create their directories at the right branches.

## Basic steps

1 Select the directory that will be the parent of your new one. This will be the root if you want to create a first level directory.

2 Open the **File** menu.

3 Select **Create Directory**

4 At the dialog box, type a suitable name – the same rules apply here as to filenames.

5 Check the tree. Is it in the right place?

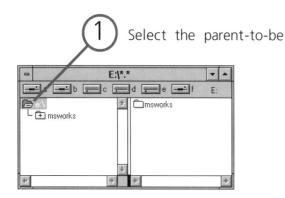

① Select the parent-to-be

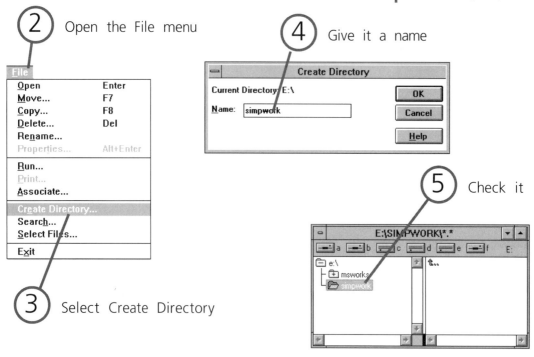

② Open the File menu

④ Give it a name

③ Select Create Directory

⑤ Check it

# Moving directories

1 Arrange the display so that you can see the directory you want to move and the place it has to move to.

2 Drag the directory to its new position, *making sure the target is outlined.*

3 Check the new tree.

Those of us who are less organised set up our new directories when the old ones get so full that it is difficult to find things. Nor do we always create them in the most suitable place in the tree. Fortunately, Windows caters for us too. Files can easily be moved from one directory to another (See Moving and copying, page 86), and directories can easily be moved to new places on the tree.

In this example, *logos* is being moved to be a branch of the *vb* directory.

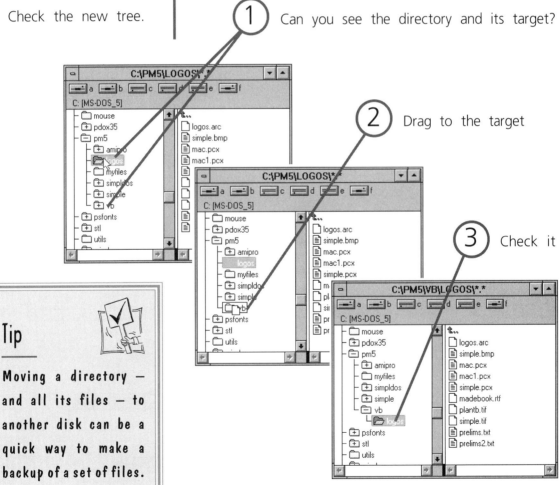

① Can you see the directory and its target?

② Drag to the target

③ Check it

## Tip

**Moving a directory — and all its files — to another disk can be a quick way to make a backup of a set of files.**

# Deleting directories

This is not something you will do every day, for deleting a directory also deletes its files, and files are usually precious things. But there are times. We all acquire programs we don't need, keep files long past their use-by dates, and sometimes create unnecessary directories.

● Do check the directory first, and move any files that you may want to a safe place first.

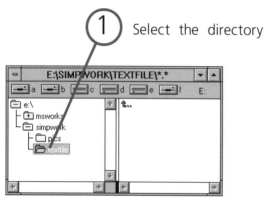

① Select the directory

1 Select the directory – and check the files list. Are there any there? Do you want any of them? No, carry on.

2 Press **[Delete]** or select **Delete** from the **File** menu.

3 Check the name in the dialog box and **OK** or **Cancel**.

4 Have a last thought before you click **Yes** in the **Confirm Delete** box.

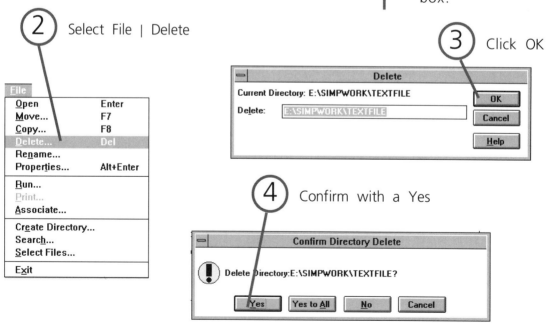

② Select File | Delete

③ Click OK

④ Confirm with a Yes

# Confirmation

## Basic steps

1 Open the **Options** menu.

2 Select **Confirmation**

3 Remove the cross from those check boxes where you do not want to have to confirm the action.

4 Click **OK**.

Windows makes things easy – sometimes too easy. The confirmation routines are there to guard against accidentally deleting or moving files and directories. Having to confirm that you really do want to delete, move, rename or copy something, may be a nuisance, but it is a small price to pay for safety.

Leave all the confirmations on at first. When you are confident of your accuracy with the mouse, you may like to turn the **Mouse Action** confirm off. **Directory Delete** should really be left on always. As to the rest, see how far they get in your way, and balance that against how much destruction and chaos they have helped to avert.

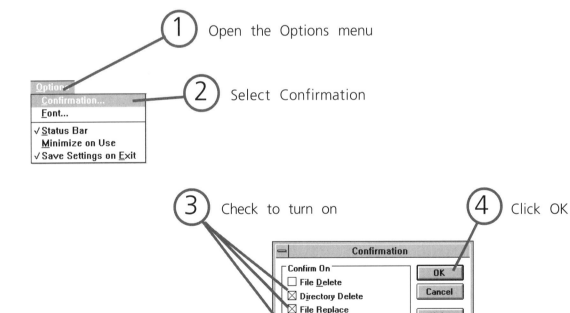

67

# Summary

❏ Disks are normally sub-divided into **directories**, to give organised storage for files.

❏ A directory's place in the tree is identified by its **path**.

❏ A **filename** has two components, the name itself and an extension.

❏ The **name** can be up to 8 characters long, and contain any mixture of letters, digits and some symbols.

❏ **Extensions** are used to identify the nature of the file.

❏ When you create a new directory, it will be placed on the branch below the selected directory.

❏ A directory, and its files, can be moved to a new position on the tree.

❏ A directory, and its files and sub-directories can be deleted – but there are two levels of confirmation to prevent this hapening accidentally.

❏ The **Confirmation** option should be turned on for those actions where there is a chance of accidental damage.

# 7 Viewing files

# Tree and Directory views

The directory windows are normally split evenly between the Tree and Directory display. This may not always suit. If there is a lot of file information that you want to see, a bigger Directory pane would held; if you are concentrating on the structure, a bigger Tree pane is useful.

You can change the balance of pane sizes by moving the dividing line.

## Basic steps

1 Move the arrow pointer over the line between the panes until the split pointer appears.

2 Hold down the left button and a thick dividing line will appear.

3 Drag the dividing line to its new position and release.

Split pointer

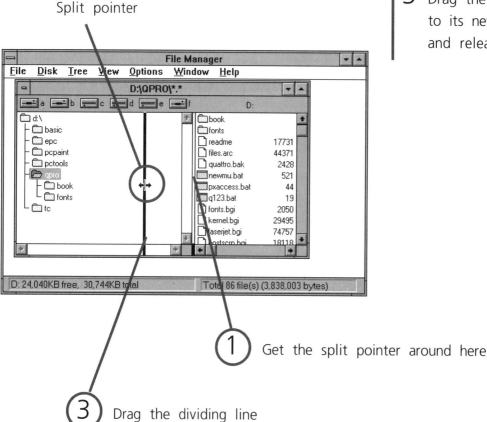

① Get the split pointer around here

③ Drag the dividing line

70

# Basic steps

1 Open the **View** menu.

2 Select either

   **Tree Only**

   or

   **Directory Only**

3 Revert to the normal **Tree and Directory** display after you have finished the job.

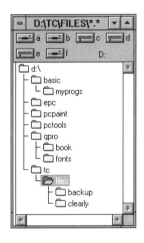

The Tree Only display

# Single-pane views

There will be times when your interest will be purely in either the Tree or Directory display, and not both. As you might well have two or more directory windows open at the time, you can avoid overlap and confusion if each window is no larger than it needs to be.

For times like this, the **Tree Only** and **Directory Only** options will reduce the display to a single pane.

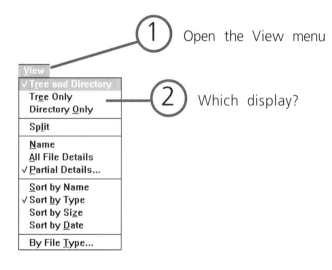

(1) Open the View menu

(2) Which display?

The Directory Only display

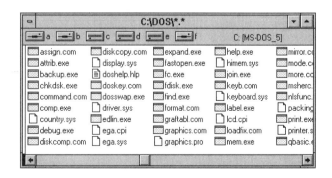

# Multiple windows

When you are moving directories or copying files from one disk or directory to another, or when you are trying to locate the scattered files that must be pulled together into a report, it is useful to be able to have more than one directory window open at a time. This is easily done – perhaps *too* easily.

● Click once on a drive icon, and you change the drive for that window.

● Double-click on a drive icon and you open a new window for that drive.

If you are heavy-handed, you can soon amass quite a collection of directory windows. Watch out for this, and be prepared to close down unwanted windows – they just clutter up the screen.

Double-click to open

Double-click to close

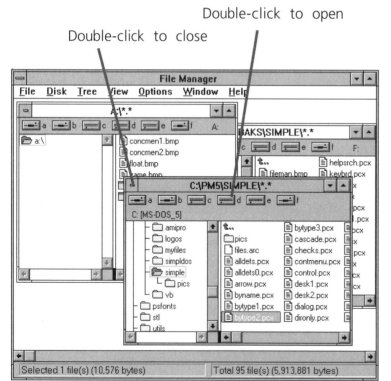

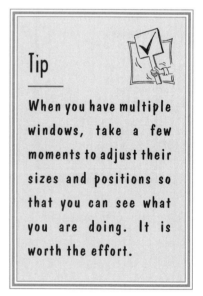

**Tip**

**When you have multiple windows, take a few moments to adjust their sizes and positions so that you can see what you are doing. It is worth the effort.**

## Basic steps

1 Open the **Options** menu.

2 Select **Font**

3 At the dialog box, select the typeface, style and size - using the Sample as a guide.

4 Click **OK**.

( 1 )  Open the Options

**Options**
| Confirmation... |
| Font... |
| √ Status Bar |
| Minimize on Use |
| √ Save Settings on Exit |

( 2 )  Select Font

# Fonts for filing

Are you having trouble reading the small print on the File Manager screen, or would you just like to give it your own personal touch? There is an option that will let you choose the type, style and size of the font used for listing the files.

● A sans serif font (one without the twiddly bits at the ends of straight lines) is generally easier to read in small sizes. Arial, Helvetica and Sans are almost always available and produce nice clear type.

● Avoid decorated typefaces like the plague. They can be good for headings or special effects, but are very tiring where there is a lot of text.

● Keep the size down to the smallest that you can read comfortably. The larger the type, the less you get in a window, and the more time you spend scrolling up and down trying to find stuff.

( 4 )  Click OK

This is in Arial, Bold, 12 point

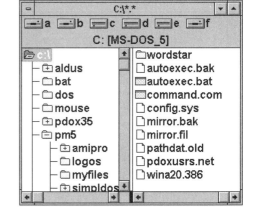

( 3 )  Set the Font, Style and Size

# Which types of files?

The normal display shows every file that is in a directory, but do you want to see them all? If you are trying to track down a program, then the data files are just clutter. If you want to get at your data files to copy them onto a back-up disk, then the prgoram files are in the way.

Windows lets you select the type of files to be displayed. There are four types:

- **Directories** – i.e. the sub-directories of the currently selected directory

- **Programs** – marked by .**com** or .**exe** after the name

- **Documents** – text, or any other sort of data files which are *associated* with particular programs. Double-clicking on them will start the program, with the file open. (See Associating files, page 92.)

- **Other files** – data files that are not associated, and overlay files that are part of software packages.

The **Hidden/System Files** are those used by MS-DOS and WIndows to run the computer. Turn the **Show** option on to see them if you like, but never move, delete or otherwise fiddle with them!

The **View** | **By Type** dialog box also allows you to select files using *wildcards*.

(See Associating files, page 92.)

## Basic steps

1 Open the **View** menu.

2 Select **By Type.**

3 When the dialog box opens, click on the check boxes to select the types you want, or deselect those you don't want to see.

or

type in a **wildcard expression** to display files that have part of their name in common.

4 Click **OK.**

(1) Open the View menu

(2) Select By Type

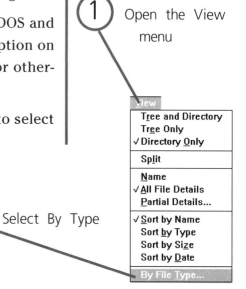

# Wildcard expressions

Wildcards are characters that can stand for any other.
Use them to select groups of files with similar names.

? stands for any single character

* stands for a string of characters

| Expression | Selected files |
|---|---|
| *.DOC | report.doc, ms2.doc, memo.doc |
| A*.* | Aardvark.pcx, amemo.doc, Alist.db |
| CHAP?.DOC | chap1.doc, chap2.doc, chap3.doc |

③ Crosses on the types you want

③ or give a wildcard expression

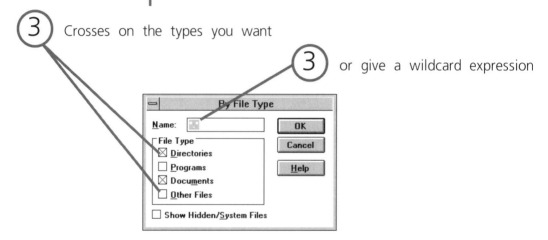

Click here to switch to the
parent directory

Program files only in a
Directory Only display.

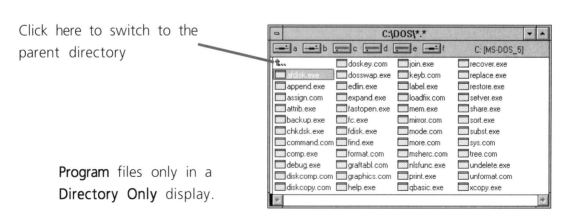

75

# Directory information

File Manager normally only lists the names of files, but it holds more detailed information about them. Sometimes you will want to see some or all of these details.

● **Size** - how many bytes of disk space the file occupies. When you are trying to free up space on a disk, this can help you to decide which ones to delete.

● **Date** and **Time** - when the file was last changed. This can help you to find files if you know when you last worked on them but have forgotten their names.

● The **Attributes** are single letter codes. Much of the time they will be of little interest to you.

**Basic steps**

1 Choose **View**.

2 Choose the level of information - **Name** (only), **All details** or **Partial details**.

3 If you choose **Partial details**, a dialog box opens. If the check box beside each detail contains a cross, it will be included in the display. Click on the box to turn the cross on or off again.

4 Press OK to save the changes.

5 Check out the display. Does it show you what you want - and can you see it all? With those extra details, you may need to adjust the size of the window.

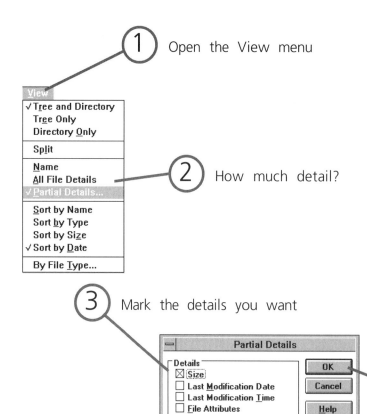

Open the View menu

How much detail?

Mark the details you want

Click OK

**76**

# Attributes

**a** Altered since the last backup was performed;

**r** Read Only - you can use the program or read the data, but the file cannot be changed or deleted;

**h** Hidden file - does not normally appear in a listing.

**S** System file - never delete one of these!

**Tip**

If any details are displayed, the files are listed one per line, so if you need to see lots of files, stick to a **Names only**

The exclamation mark indicates that a file is usually hidden. Hiding a file is a good way to prevent it from being accidentally deleted, which is why the Windows and DOS systems hide their essential files.

These are only visible if you have checked the **Show Hidden/System Files** in the **View By Type** dialog box.

Check the display

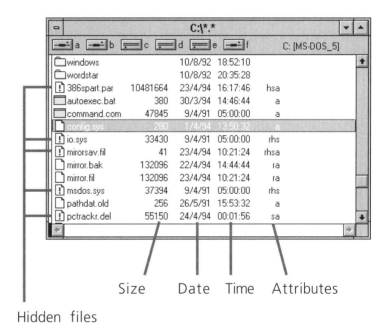

Hidden files · Size · Date · Time · Attributes

**Date** and **Time** refer to the last time that the file was saved. Simply reading a file will not affect this.

# Sorting files

If a directory is sorted into order, it makes it easier to find files and to select them for copying, deleting or other operations. There are four possible sorts:

- by Name  simple alphabetical order;

- by Type  groups those with the same extension, with each group sorted by name order;

- by Size  largest first – very useful when you want to clear some space or are trying to work out what files you can fit on a floppy disk

- by Date  (and Time) latest first.

**By Type** is probably the most useful. Combined with a Name only display, it gives you a compact grouping of related files for copying operations.

## Basic steps

❑ **Sorting by Type**

1 Open the **View** menu

2 Select **Sort by Type**

3 Scroll through the directory list to see the set of files that interests you.

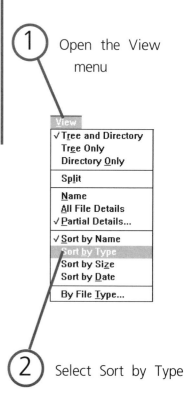

1 Open the View menu

2 Select Sort by Type

3 Scroll through the directory list

# Basic steps

1 Open the **View** menu

2 Select **Partial Details**

3 Check the **Date** and **Time** boxes

4 Open the **View** menu again and select **Sort by Date**

5 Scroll through to the relevant time.

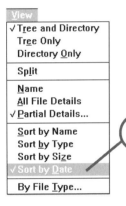

# Sorting by date

This is best used combined with the Date and Time details display. Together they can help you to identify the latest version of a file and to find those where you can remember when you last used them, but not what they were called – a not unusual situation!

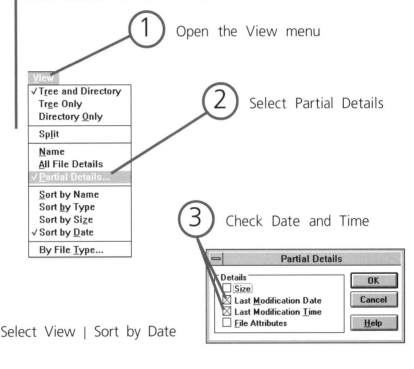

① Open the View menu

② Select Partial Details

③ Check Date and Time

④ Select View | Sort by Date

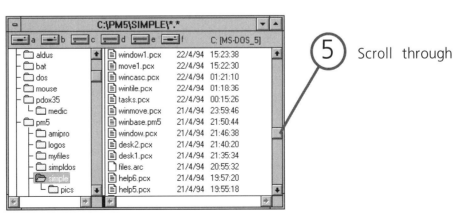

⑤ Scroll through

# Searching for a file

Most of the time you will know exactly where all your files are, because you will have stored them in the appropriate directories. Sometimes the system fails and you will forget to check the directory before saving a file. Sometimes you will be looking for a file that another person saved somewhere, or one that came with a package.

**Search** is for times like these. It will find a named file, or a file that matches a wildcard expression. Starting from any selected point in the tree, it hunts through all the branches below and lists the paths of any files that match your specifications.

In the example given here, I am looking for a file called *accounts*, or *accounts.txt* or something similar. Notice the * wildcard that will stand for any extension. You might also notice from the results window, that the search revealed four different files. There is a lesson here about making filenames meaningful and specific. I shall have to look at all four to find my accounts for 1992-93!

## Basic steps

1 Select the directory at the top of the branch you want to search.

2 Open the **File** menu.

3 Select **Search**.

4 At the dialog box type in the filename or a wildcard expression.

5 Wait for the **Search Results** window.

**Tip**

The root is always a good place to start. It only takes a few seconds longer to search the whole disk, and you are sure to find it if it is there — somewhere.

① Select the start point

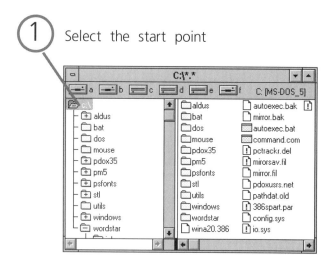

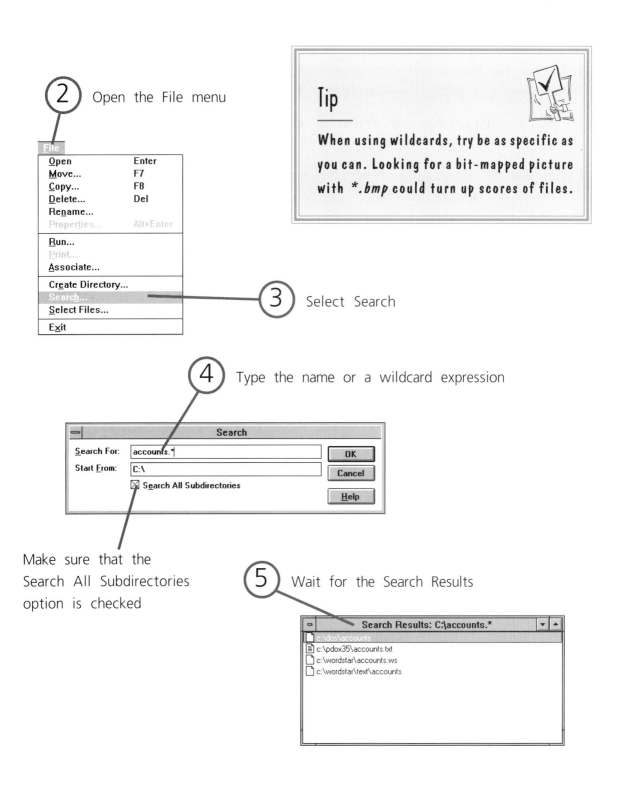

(2) Open the File menu

**File**

| | |
|---|---|
| **Open** | Enter |
| **Move...** | F7 |
| **Copy...** | F8 |
| **Delete...** | Del |
| **Rename...** | |
| Properties... | Alt+Enter |
| **Run...** | |
| Print... | |
| **Associate...** | |
| **Create Directory...** | |
| Search... | |
| **Select Files...** | |
| E**x**it | |

(3) Select Search

## Tip

When using wildcards, try be as specific as you can. Looking for a bit-mapped picture with *.bmp could turn up scores of files.

(4) Type the name or a wildcard expression

**Search**

| Search For: | accounts.* | | OK |
|---|---|---|---|
| Start From: | C:\ | | Cancel |
| | ☒ Search All Subdirectories | | Help |

Make sure that the
Search All Subdirectories
option is checked

(5) Wait for the Search Results

**Search Results: C:\accounts.***

c:\dos\accounts
c:\pdox35\accounts.txt
c:\wordstar\accounts.ws
c:\wordstar\text\accounts

# Summary

❑ The File Manager display can show either or both of the Tree structure and the **Directory** list of files.

❑ You can open windows for several directories at once.

❑ The **Font** option lets you change the appearance and size of the print. Use this if you have difficulty reading the displays.

❑ You can specify which **Types** of files are to be shown, and the level of **Details** about those files.

❑ Wildcards can be used to stand for any characters, if you want to select a set of files, or find one when you are not sure of the name.

❑ The files in the directory list can be sorted by **Name**, **Type**, **Size** or **Date.**

❑ When sorting files, include the Details that you are sorting on, in the display.

❑ The **Search** facility will hunt through all the branches of the tree to find lost files for you.

# 8  Managing files

# Selecting sets of files

As well as being able to select a single file, you can also select groups of files. This comes in useful when you want to backup a day's work by copying the new files to a floppy disk, or move a group from one directory to another, or delete a load of files that are not wanted.

There are three ways in which you can select a group.

- With **[Shift]** you can select a block of adjacent files;

- With **[Ctrl]** you can select a scattered set;

- With the **Select Files** command you can pick out a set that matches a wildcard expression.

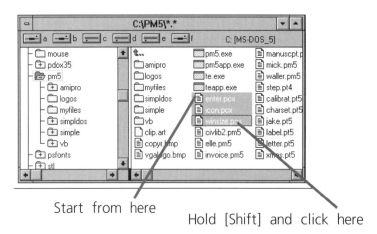

Start from here

Hold [Shift] and click here

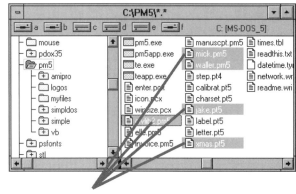

Hold [Ctrl] while you click

❏ **To select a block of files**

**1** Use a **View | Sort** option to bring the files together.

**2** Click on the file at one end of the block.

**3** If necessary, scroll the window to bring the end of the block into view.

**4** Hold **[Shift]** and click on the far end file.

❏ You can reselect the far end file, but the first cannot be changed without starting again.

❏ **To select scattered files**

**1** Click on any one of the files you want.

**2** Hold **[Ctrl]** and click each of the other files in turn.

❏ You can deselect any file by clicking on it a second time.

## Basic steps

1 Open the **File** menu.

2 Choose **Select Files**

3 Type in a wildcard expression.

4 Click **Close**.

5 If the wildcard has selected more than you want, go back into **Select Files**.

6 Type a new expression that will pick out the files you do **not** want.

7 Click **Deselect**, then **Close**.

## Select Files

The **File | Select Files** command will find those in the current directory that match a wildcard expression. The default for this is *.* – use that if you want to select *all* the files.

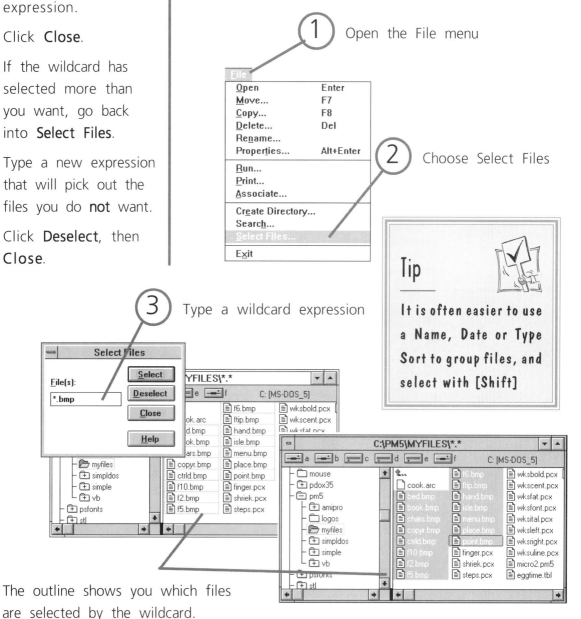

① Open the File menu

② Choose Select Files

③ Type a wildcard expression

**Tip**

It is often easier to use a Name, Date or Type Sort to group files, and select with [Shift]

The outline shows you which files are selected by the wildcard.

# Moving and copying

When you drag a file from one place to another, it will either move or copy the file. What happens depends upon where you drag it to.

It is a **move** if you drag to somewhere *on the same disk.*

It is a **copy** if you drag the file *to a different disk.*

This is generally right. When you are dragging files within a disk, it is usually a move to reorganised your storage, and copying is most commonly to create a security backup, and there is no security on the same disk.

Sometimes you do want to copy within a disk, or move between them. There are commands to deal with these situations.

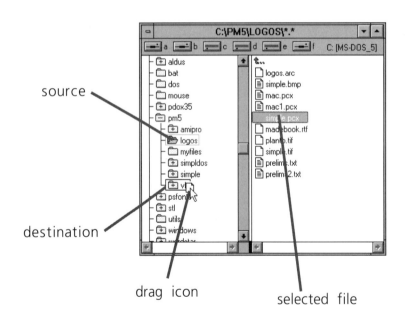

source

destination

drag icon

selected file

❑ **Moving within a disk**

1 Arrange your **File Manager** display so that you can see the source and destination directories.

2 Select the file(s) to be moved.

3 Point to any of the selected files and drag the icon to the destination directory.

❑ **Copying between disks**

1 Arrange your **File Manager** display so that you can see the directories on both disks.

2 Select the file(s) and drag to the destination.

source directory

selected file

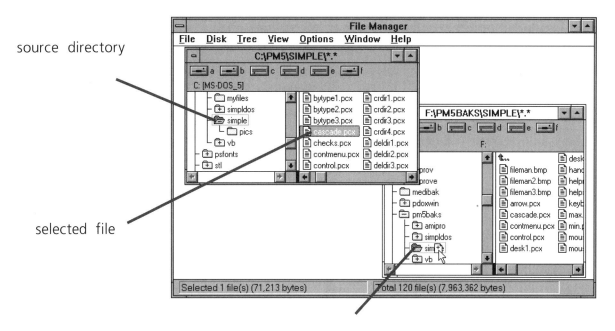

destination directory

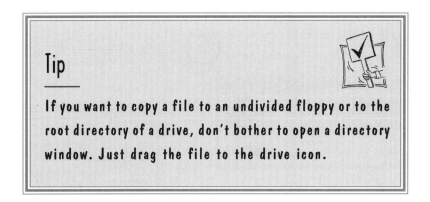

## Tip

If you want to copy a file to an undivided floppy or to the root directory of a drive, don't bother to open a directory window. Just drag the file to the drive icon.

87

# File | Move and File | Copy

Use these commands when you want to **move** files and directories *between* drives, and **copy** them *within* the same drive. Both are used in the same way.

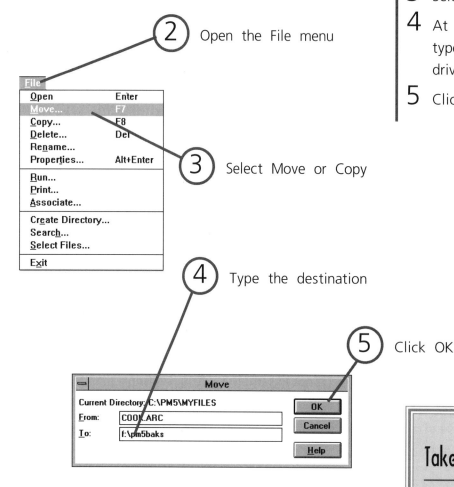

(2) Open the File menu

(3) Select Move or Copy

(4) Type the destination

(5) Click OK

## Basic steps

1 Select the file (or directory).

2 Open the **File** menu.

3 Select **Move** or **Copy**.

4 At the dialog box, type in the destination drive and directory.

5 Click **OK**

## Take note

To copy a file in the same directory, type in a new filename and omit the drive/directory path.

## Basic steps

1 Select the file (or directory).

2 Open the **File** menu.

3 Select **Rename**.

4 At the dialog box, type in the new name.

5 Click **OK**

# Renaming a file

This is another command from the same stable as File|Move and File|Copy. Renaming a file is equivalent to moving it and changing its name. It can only be done with the **Rename** option on the **File** menu.

At the dialog box, include the drive/directory path only if you want to move it while you rename it.

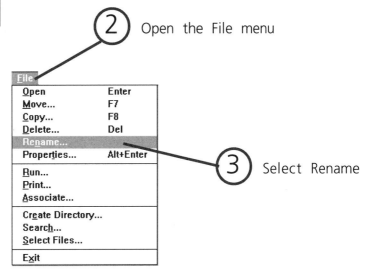

② Open the File menu

③ Select Rename

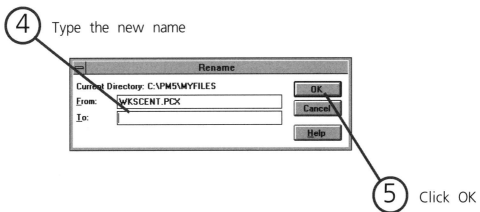

④ Type the new name

⑤ Click OK

# Deleting files

Play safe! Make sure that the **Confirm File Delete** option is turned on before you even think about deleting files. MSDOS does have an UNDELETE program that you can use to recover files (sometimes), but there is no easy way of correcting a Delete mistake from within Windows.

1 Select the file, or group of files.

2 Press **[Delete]**.

3 Check the name(s) at the dialog box and either **OK** or **Cancel** the delete.

4 At the **Confirm** dialog box, use **Yes** and **No** to confirm each individual file, or **Yes to All** to confirm the deletion of the whole group.

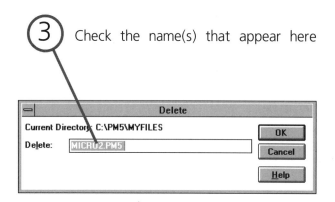

③ Check the name(s) that appear here

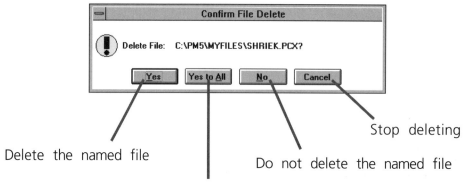

Stop deleting

Delete the named file

Do not delete the named file

Delete a whole group of files

## Tip

**To find out more about Undelete (and other DOS utilities) read MS-DOS Made Simple.**

## Basic steps

1 Select the program in the File Manager display.

2 Open the **File** menu.

3 Select **Run**.

4 At the dialog box, edit the command line to add the filename, directory or other argument.

5 Click **OK**.

You can run a program from File Manager simply by double-clicking on its name. The effect is the same as if you had typed its name in at the DOS prompt.

Sometimes when starting a program, you have to type an *argument* after the name. This argument might be the name of a file that you want the program to work on, or the directory you want to work in, or it might be a special code that makes the program work ina particular way. At times like these, you should use the **File | Run** approach. This calls up a dialog box in which you can type the arguments after the program name.

## Take note

If you select **Run Minimized**, the program will start with its window reduced to an icon. You can then **Restore** it, as and when you need it during the session.

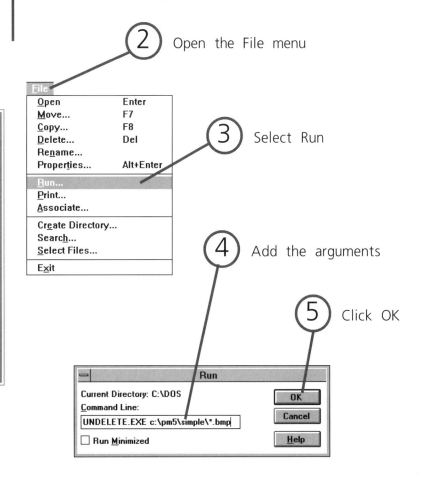

② Open the File menu

③ Select Run

④ Add the arguments

⑤ Click OK

| File | |
|---|---|
| Open | Enter |
| Move... | F7 |
| Copy... | F8 |
| Delete... | Del |
| Rename... | |
| Properties... | Alt+Enter |
| **Run...** | |
| Print... | |
| Associate... | |
| Create Directory... | |
| Search... | |
| Select Files... | |
| Exit | |

**Run**

Current Directory: C:\DOS
Command Line:
UNDELETE.EXE c:\pm5\simple\*.bmp

☐ Run Minimized

OK
Cancel
Help

# Associating files

An associated file is one that is linked to a program, so that clicking on the file runs the program, and opens up that data file. Windows refers to them as *Documents*, and they can be recognised by their 📄 icons, as distinct from the 🗋 icons of unassociated files.

If you only use proper Windows applications, you won't ever have to bother about this, because the applications take care of the associating.

If you are using a DOS program – perhaps brought into Program Manger as shown in Adding a new item, page 54 – then you may want to associate files with it.

page 54

## Basic steps

1 Select a file which has the right extension.

2 Open the **File** menu

3 Select **Associate**.

4 At the dialog box, select the program file from the list if it is present, otherwise click on **Browse**.

5 Browse to the right drive and directory.

6 Select the program file.

7 Click **OK**.

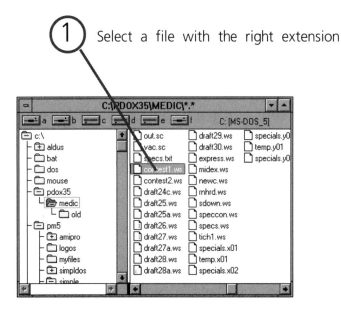

① Select a file with the right extension

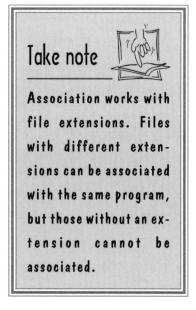

## Take note

Association works with file extensions. Files with different extensions can be associated with the same program, but those without an extension cannot be associated.

**92**

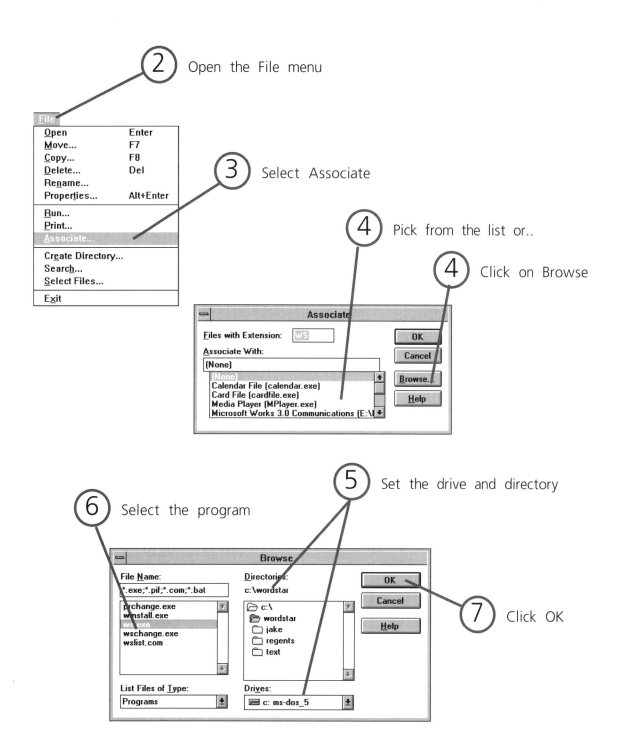

② Open the File menu

③ Select Associate

④ Pick from the list or..

④ Click on Browse

⑤ Set the drive and directory

⑥ Select the program

⑦ Click OK

**File**

| | |
|---|---|
| Open | Enter |
| Move... | F7 |
| Copy... | F8 |
| Delete... | Del |
| Rename... | |
| Properties... | Alt+Enter |
| Run... | |
| Print... | |
| Associate... | |
| Create Directory... | |
| Search... | |
| Select Files... | |
| Exit | |

**Associate**

Files with Extension: WS

Associate With:

[None]

[None]
Calendar File (calendar.exe)
Card File (cardfile.exe)
Media Player (MPlayer.exe)
Microsoft Works 3.0 Communications (E:\)

OK
Cancel
Browse...
Help

**Browse**

File Name:
*.exe;*.pif;*.com;*.bat

prchange.exe
winstall.exe
ws.exe
wschange.exe
wslist.com

List Files of Type:
Programs

Directories:
c:\wordstar

c:\
wordstar
jake
regents
text

Drives:
c: ms-dos_5

OK
Cancel
Help

93

# Installing programs

## Windows Software

When you buy a new Windows application it should have an installation program. This is normally on the first of the supplied disks and is usually called INSTALL or SETUP. You should only have to run that program and follow its on-screen instructions. While you sit and feed in disks when asked, the program will do everything for you – set up directories, copy files and create an icon and a group.

## DOS Software

Most DOS applications also have an installation program that will handle everything apart from bringing the software into Program Manager.

If there is no installation program, check the software's documentation for guidance, then make the directories and copy in the files.

If you have neither documentation nor installation instructions, then create a suitably named directory and drag each disk into it. This will retain any sub-directory structure while copying in the files.

### Basic steps

❏ DIY Installation

1 Create a directory, giving it a suitable name.

2 Open a directory window for Drive A: and one for the target hard disk (usually C:).

3 Select the root directory of the A: drive.

4 Drag the directory to the target direct.

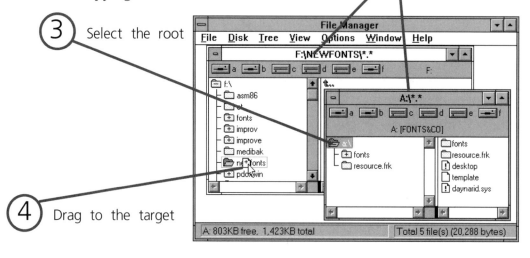

② Open windows for both directories

③ Select the root

④ Drag to the target

94

# Basic steps

1 Adjust the File Manager window so that you can see the Program Manager group into which the item will go.

2 Open the directory containing the program and select the main EXE file.

3 Drag the program file into its new group.

## Adding by dragging

Once installed, a DOS program can be brought into Windows by dragging its file icon into a Program Manager group. This is often quicker than the **File | New** method shown in Adding a new item (page 54). Refer back to that if you want to adjust its Properties or change its icon.

If the program does not work properly under Windows, you may have to adjust its PIF – Program Information File. (See Editing a PIF, page121.)

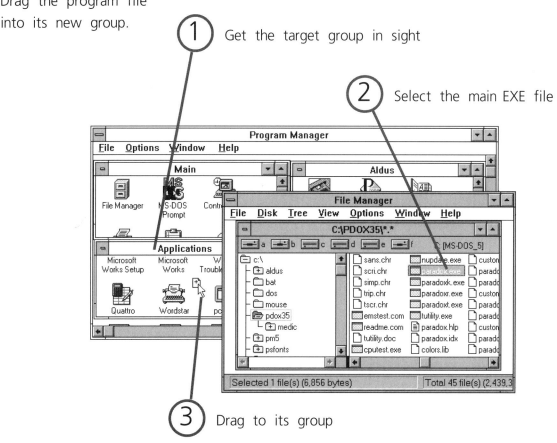

① Get the target group in sight

② Select the main EXE file

③ Drag to its group

# Summary

❑ Groups of files can be selected by holding **[Shift]** or **[Ctrl]** while clicking on filenames

❑ **File | Select** can be used to select a group that matches a wildcard expression.

❑ A selected file or set of files can be moved or copied be dragging the icon from one directory to another.

❑ To move a file from one disk to another, use **File | Move**.

❑ To copy a file within the same disk, use **Flle | Copy**.

❑ **File | Rename** will change the name of a file, or move it to a different directory with a new name.

❑ Selected files can be deleted by pressing **[Delete]**. If the **Confirm File Delete** option is on, you will re-duce the chande of deleting files by mistake.

❑ Programs can be run by clicking on their icons, or with **File | Run**. This method allows you to add filenames or other arguments to the command line.

❑ **Associated** data files are linked to programs, so that clicking on the file icon runs the program.

❑ Installing new software is usually easy, thanks to the installation programs that are part of most modern packages.

# 9 Floppy disks

# Formatting a floppy

Before you can use a new floppy disk, it is must be **formatted**. This is a process of marking out magnetic tracks on the disk surface, to divide the blank area up into numbered blocks to provide organised storage space.

The **Disk | Format** command takes the hard work out of this – all you have to do is make sure that you know what kind of disk you are formatting.

PC disks come in two sizes and four capacities.

  5˜ inch 360Kb Double-Density (DD)

  5˜ inch 1.2Mb High-Density (HD)

  3° inch 730Kb Double-Density (DD)

  3° inch 1.44Mb High-Density (HD)

Modern PC are fitted with drives that can take either of the 3° inch disks. The 1.44Mb disk is generally better value for money.

## Basic steps

1  Insert the disk into the drive.

2  Open the **Disk** menu

3  Select **Format Disk**

4  At the dialog box, make sure that it is working with the right drive and disk size.

5  Click **OK**

6  Confirm that you mean it.

7  Wait a bit - it takes around a minute to format a 1.44Mb disk.

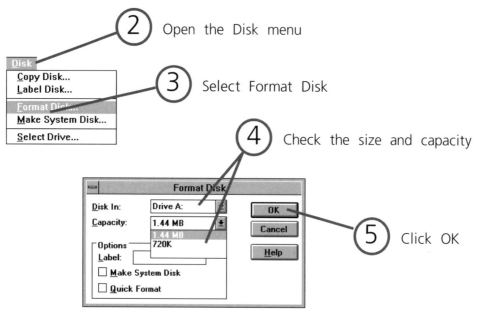

② Open the Disk menu

③ Select Format Disk

④ Check the size and capacity

⑤ Click OK

# Caring for floppies

Disk drives can be mounted horizontally or vertically, but a disk will only go in one way round. If it won't fit, don't force it. Try it the other way round.

The modern 3° floppy is a far tougher beast than the older 5˘ ones. Its plastic casing protects it well against grime, knocks and splashes of coffee, but it still has enemies. Heat, damp and magnetism will both go through the casing and corrupt the data on the disk beneath. So, keep your disks away from radiators, sunny windowsills, magnets, heavy electrical machinery or mains cables (both produce magnetic fields.)

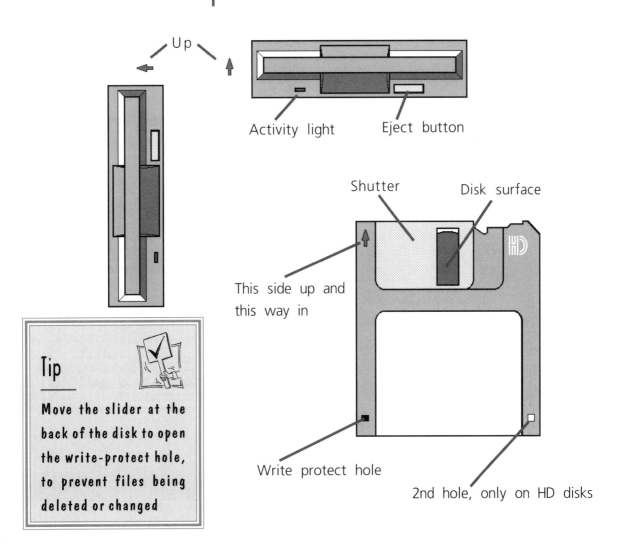

Up

Activity light     Eject button

Shutter     Disk surface

This side up and this way in

Write protect hole

2nd hole, only on HD disks

## Tip

Move the slider at the back of the disk to open the write-protect hole, to prevent files being deleted or changed

# Making a system disk

A system disk is one that contains the essential files that are needed to start up, or *boot*, the computer. These are present on the hard disk, but there is always the chance that one day some or all of those files will be deleted by accident, or even that the hard disk will develop problems. Having a bootable floppy disk is an essential piece of insurance. If you have a system disk in drive A: when you turn the PC on, it will start up using the files it finds there. You can then restore your deleted files or try to recover files from the hard disk.

File Manager offers two ways of making a system disk. This simplest method is usually to take the **Make System Disk** option on the **Format Disk** dialog box.

## Basic steps

1 Follow the initial steps for formatting a floppy (see previous page.)

2 Turn on the **Make System Disk** option.

3 Wait for disk to be formatted and files to be copied.

4 Check that they are there by turning on the **Show Hidden Files** option on the **View | By File Type** menu.

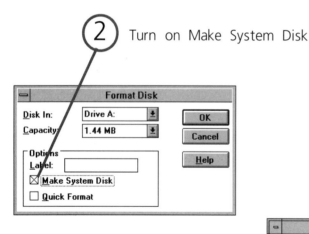

② Turn on Make System Disk

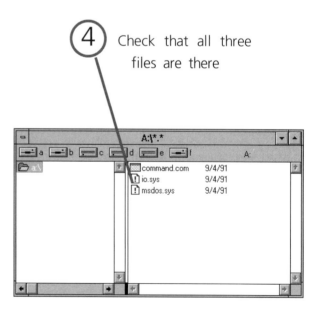

④ Check that all three files are there

# Basic steps

1 Insert a blank formatted disk into a drive - normally drive A:
2 Open the **Disk** menu.
3 Select **Make System Disk**
4 Select the drive if necessary.
5 Wait for files to be copied.

## Tip

Copy your Autoexec.bat and Config.sys files onto your system disk. You will need a backup copy of these if your hard disk files do get deleted.

# Copying system files

The second method may seem to be the obvious one to use, but it is not always the best. There is a menu option **Disk | Make System Disk**, but all it does is copy the system files. The disk must be formatted already, and it must be completely blank.

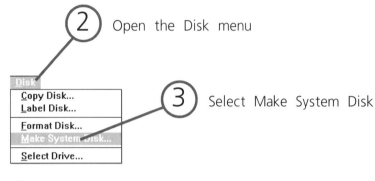

② Open the Disk menu

③ Select Make System Disk

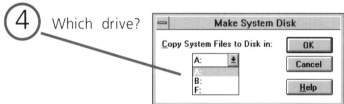

④ Which drive?

# The system files

These are the files that make DOS work, and Windows can only work if DOS is already up and running.

**Command.com** contains the core DOS commands for controlling the PC and the file storage.

**Msdos.sys** and **Io.sys** contain low-level routines for managing the hardware. These are both hidden files.

**Dblspace.bin** will be present if you use the Double-Space disk utility.

# Disk copying

When you buy a new application package, the first thing you should do is copy all the master disks. These are then put into a safe place, and the installation is done from the copied floppies. This is insurance. If something goes wrong during installation (highly unlikely, but possible), then at least you won't have corrupted the original disks.

For this job, and for other times when you want to copy all the files on the disk, you should use **Copy Disk**.

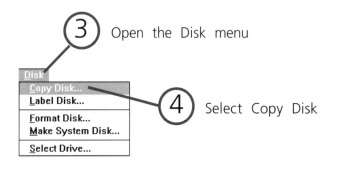

③ Open the Disk menu

④ Select Copy Disk

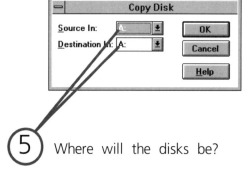

⑤ Where will the disks be?

## Take note

**You can only use Copy Disk to copy files onto another disk of the same size and capacity.**

## Basic steps

1 Have your source and spare disk(s) to hand. The ones that are to be copied onto do not have to be blank, nor do they have to be formatted, but *they must be the same capacity as the source disks*.

2 Place the source disk into the drive.

3 Open the **Disk** menu.

4 Select **Copy Disk**

5 At the dialog box, tell it where the source and destination disks will be. They will usually both be in the same drive – one after the other.

**6** Change the disks when prompted.

**7** Stick a label on the new copy and write down what it is.

**8** If you are copying a set of master disks, go back to Step 2 with the next floppy.

❑ Do not get your source and destination disks confused!

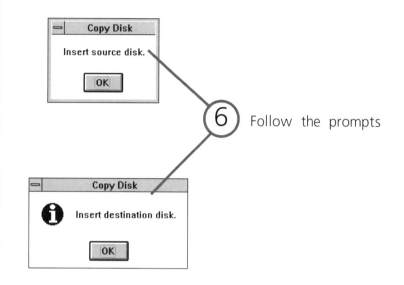

**6** Follow the prompts

**Tip**

If you close the write protect hole on the source disks, they cannot possibly be written over, even if you get the source and destination piles mixed up.

**Copy Disk** keeps you informed of progress. Be ready to swap disks at around 50%.

If the destination disk is not formatted, Copy Disk will take care of that.

**103**

# Summary

❑ Floppy disks come in two sizes and four storage capacities. Modern PCs take either of the 3˚ inch disks.

❑ Floppies must be **formatted** before they can be used for storage.

❑ Floppies should be stored somewhere cool, dry and free from magnetic fields.

❑ You should make one floppy into a **system disk**, in case the core MS-DOS files get deleted from the hard disk, or the hard disk crashes.

❑ The quickest way to copy all the files from a floppy to another (of the same type), is with **Copy Disk**.

# 10 Print Manager

# What does it do?

Print Manager

Print Manager handles all aspects of printing in Windows. This is where you install a new printer, and decide which one to use. And when you send a file for printing, it goes to a queue within Print Manager, rather than heading straight for the printer.

PCs can output files faster than printers can get them onto paper. A buffer (temporary storage) in the printer will help to smooth out the difference, but buffers are not that large. They range from a few Kilobytes in an old dot-matrix, up to a couple of Megabytes in a laser printer. A word-processed or DTP'd report may well generate several Megabytes of data. If this is being sent directly to the printer, the PC – and you – could spend quite a while waiting for the printer to churn it out.

The **print queue** is a neat solution to this problem. When the word-processor, or other application, 'prints' a document, it is taken by the Print Manager and stored on the hard disk as a file, ready formatted for the printer. Once the application has finished sending the file, it is free for other work, while Print Manager deals with the printer. It does this *in the background*, grabbing a little of the processor's time every now and then to send another chunk of data to the printer. It slows down the system a little, but at least things don't grind to a halt completely.

Note that this is a *queue*, which means that it can store a whole set of files for later printing. If you like, you can delete files from the queue, or change the order in which they are dealt with. (See Managing the queue, page 112.)

---

## Take note

Print Manager is set running automatically when you send a file for printng, and as long as things are going well, you can ignore it. You will only have to bother with it are when you are setting up a printer or actively managing the queue.

## Basic steps

1 From Program Manager, click on the **Print Manager** icon (in the Main group).

2 Open the **Options** menu.

3 Set the **Priority** at the level you want.

Start it up

Print Manager

## Tip

To work out the best messaging level, set it first to Alert Always and see how it goes over the next few sessions. If it is too intrusive, try the next level down.

# Setting options

The **Options** in Print Manager determine how it interacts with you and with other applications.

The higher the **Priority**, the more processor time is taken by Print Manager when it has jobs to do. With Low Priority, other applications will run faster, but printing may be delayed. I leave mine at Medium, occasionally pushing it to high when there is a lot of printing to be done in a hurry – and not much else.

The second block of options control how Print Manager informs you of **messages** from the printer. These are not particularly important. If there are crucial problems – the printer off-line or out of paper – messages will get through whatever the setting.

Open the Options menu

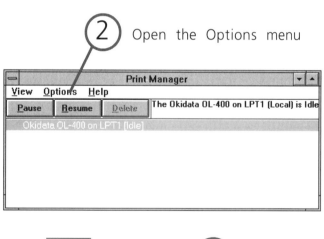

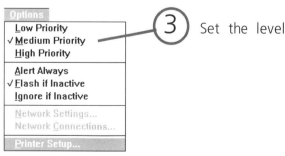

Set the level

# Installing a printer

Before you can use a printer, it must be installed into the PC, by loading in a driver – a program that controls how the printer formats text and produces graphics. A wide range of drivers are included in the Windows package These cover most printers. If you have a very new model, it should have a driver supplied with it, and if not one can normally be obtained from Microsoft.

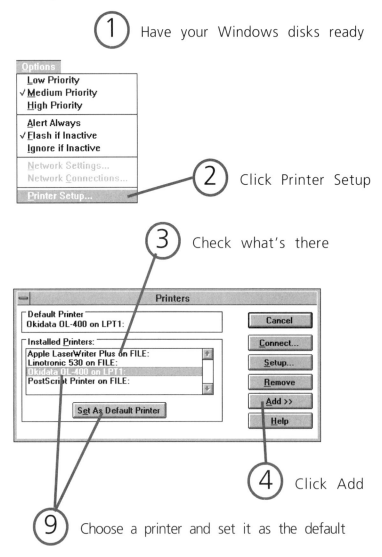

(1) Have your Windows disks ready

(2) Click Printer Setup

(3) Check what's there

(4) Click Add

(9) Choose a printer and set it as the default

1 Dig out your Windows distribution disks.

2 Open the **Options** menu and select **Printer Setup**

3 At the dialog box, check to see if you have a suitable driver already. If so, stop.

4 Choose **Add.** A new panel opens at the bottom of the box.

5 Scroll through the list to find your printer.

6 Click **Install**.

7 You will be asked to put a particular disk in Drive A:. Find it, put it in and click **OK**.

8 To install another driver, return to step 4.

9 Select your main printer from the top list and click **Set As Default**.

❑ Don't close the **Printers** dialog box yet. We haven't done with it.

# Printing elsewhere

If you want to print on a printer attached to another PC, install a driver for it and Connect it to print *to file*. (See next pages.) When you send the document for 'printing', it will be stored on a disk with all its formatting information. This file can then be output to paper from the other PC with the DOS PRINT command.

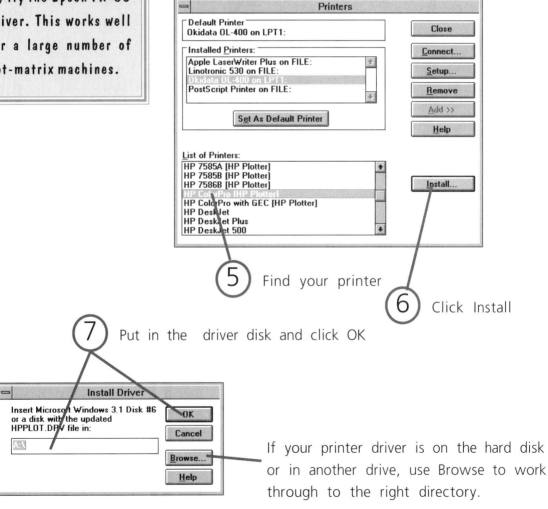

**Tip**

If you have a very old or unusual printer, and cannot find a driver for it, try the Epson FX-80 driver. This works well for a large number of dot-matrix machines.

⑤ Find your printer

⑥ Click Install

⑦ Put in the driver disk and click OK

If your printer driver is on the hard disk or in another drive, use Browse to work through to the right directory.

# Connecting a printer

In most cases you won't have to bother about this. At the back of the PC are a number of ports (sockets) to which the printer could be connected. Its cable is usually plugged into the one known to the PC as LPT1 – and this is usually marked *Printer*. If your printer works, ignore the rest of this. Read on if:

●     you are using a different port, or

●     you have a second printer attached, or

●     you want to print to file

●     nothing ever seems to reach your printer.

 Select your port

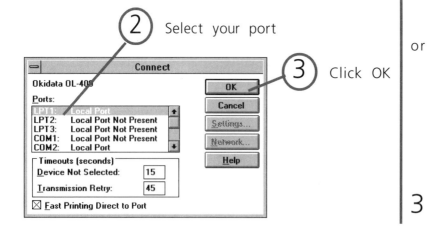

③ Click OK

Look in your printer manual to find the right settings.

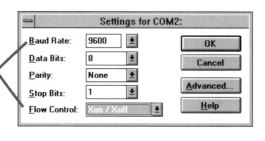

1   Open the **Printer Setup** dialog box and select **Connect**.

2   If you are using the port labelled *Printer*, select **LPT1** from the list. If it still won't work, seek expert help!

or

    If you want to create print-formatted files, select **FILE**.

or

    If you have a serial printer, select **COM2** (or COM1 – it varies) then click Settings and fill in the details there.

3   Click OK

## Basic steps

1 Open the **Printer Setup** dialog box and select **Setup**.

2 Check and adjust the settings.

❑ **Resolution** is in dots per inch. The more you have, the better the image, and the slower the printing.

❑ **Paper size** is normally A4 for cut sheets and Letter 8° x 11 for continuous stationery.

❑ **Memory** only applies if you have extra RAM in your printer.

❑ **Orientation** should be set to **Landscape** if you want to print a long image sideways.

## Take note

These settings can also be adjusted from within your applications before you print a document.

# Setting up

After you have installed the driver, the next stage is to run the Setup routine to fine tune the way the printer works. You will have to come back into this if you change the paper size, or want to print sideways or at a different resolution.

The Setup dialog box varies according to the type of printer. The ones shown here are for an OKI laser and an Epson FX-80.

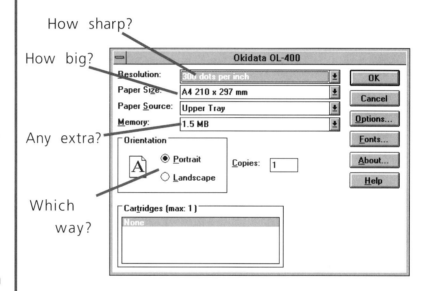

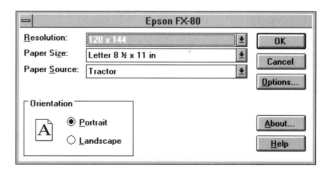

# Managing the queue

When you send a file for printing, Print Manager will automatically swing into action, and if all is going well, it can be left to its own devices. The only visible signs of its activity should be its icon at the bottom of the screen and a steady stream of paper from the printer.

If you want to cancel the printing of a document, or you have sent a whole stack and would like to change the order in which they are printed, or if you would just like to see what's going on, it is easy to get at, and easy to control.

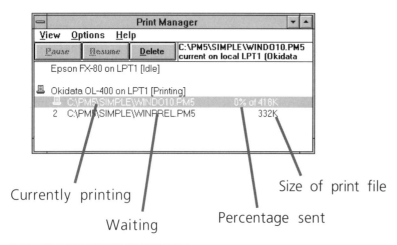

Currently printing

Waiting

Percentage sent

Size of print file

## Basic steps

❑ **To change the order**

1 Select the file you want to move.

2 Drag the file up or down to its new position.

❑ **To cancel printing a file**

1 Select the file.

2 Press **[Delete]**.

❑ **To cancel *all* printing**

1 Pull down the **View** menu.

2 Select **Exit**. You will be asked to confirm that you want to stop printing.

## Take note

Pause will stop any more data being sent to out, but the printer will continue to work on what it has already received.

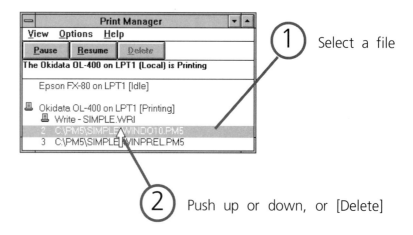

1 Select a file

2 Push up or down, or [Delete]

## Basic steps

1 Open the **View** menu.

2 Make sure the **Print File Size** option is ticked.

3 Select **Time/Date Sent** if you also want this information.

## Viewing the queue

You can change the amount of detail displayed in the Print Manager queue, just as you can in a File Manager directory. It can be left as a bare names only, or include the Time/Date Sent and Print File Size. Time and Date is rarely useful, but the Size information often is. You can use it to check on whether or not a large file is likely to swamp the printer's memory, and to estimate how long it will take to print the ones in the queue.

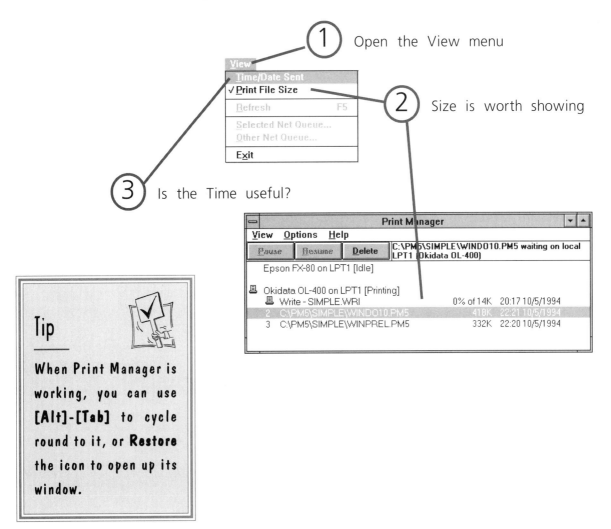

① Open the View menu

② Size is worth showing

③ Is the Time useful?

**View**
| |
|---|
| **Time/Date Sent** |
| √ Print File Size |
| Refresh      F5 |
| Selected Net Queue... |
| Other Net Queue... |
| Exit |

Print Manager

View   Options   Help

| Pause | Resume | Delete | C:\PM5\SIMPLE\WIND010.PM5 waiting on local LPT1 (Okidata OL-400) |

Epson FX-80 on LPT1 [Idle]

Okidata OL-400 on LPT1 [Printing]
  Write - SIMPLE.WRI                    0% of 14K   20:17 10/5/1994
  2   C:\PM5\SIMPLE\WIND010.PM5          418K   22:21 10/5/1994
  3   C:\PM5\SIMPLE\WINPREL.PM5          332K   22:20 10/5/1994

## Tip

When **Print Manager** is working, you can use **[Alt]-[Tab]** to cycle round to it, or **Restore** the icon to open up its window.

# Summary

❑ **Print Manager** handles all aspects of printing in WIndows

❑ Once files have been sent ot Print Manager, they are printed in the *background*, while you can get on with other jobs.

❑ The **Priority** setting determines how time is shared between the Print Manager and your current application.

❑ **Installing** a printer is usually just a matter of loading in the right driver.

❑ With **serial** printers, or where there are two attached to the PC, you will also have to set the **Connect** options.

❑ The **Set Up** options fine tune the working of the printer. These options can also be accessed from most applications, as part of their print routines.

❑ Files are stored in a **queue** before printing. You can change their order, or delete them if necessary.

❑ The **Print File Size** information is worth including in your queue display.

# 11 Useful tools

# The Clipboard

The Clipboard is a mechanism for copying and moving text, graphics and other types of data within and between documents. Whatever you are doing in Windows, it is always at hand and is used in the same way – almost.

Any Windows application that handles data or text in any form has an Edit menu. This always contains three core options – Cut, Copy and Paste – plus varying others. You can see these on the two Edit menus shown below.

● **Cut** removes a selected block of text or object, and transfers it to the Clipboard's memory.

● **Copy** takes a copy of the selected item into the Clipboard, but without removing it.

● **Paste** copies whatever is in the Clipboard into the current cursor position in the application.

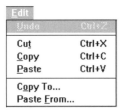

The Edit menus from Paintbrush (left) and Write (below). The core options are always there.

Take note

**Cut and Copy are only available after you have selected something. Paste is only available if there is something in the Clipboard**

## Basic steps

❑ **To Cut to the Clipboard**

1 Select the text or object.

2 Open the **Edit** menu.

3 Click **Cut**.

❑ **To Copy to the Clipboard**

1 Select the text or object.

2 Open the **Edit** menu.

3 Click **Copy**.

❑ **To Paste from the Clipboard**

1 With *text*, place the text cursor at the point where you want it to be inserted.

2 Open the **Edit** menu.

3 Click **Paste**.

4 With *graphics*, you should now move the new, selected object to where you want it to go.

# Basic steps

## ❏ To select text

1 Place the text cursor at the start of the block.

2 Drag the pointer to spread a highlight over the block.

3 You are ready to Cut or Copy.

## ❏ To select one object

1 Click on it to get handles around its edges.

## ❏ To select a set of adjacent objects

1 Imagine a rectangle that will enclose all the objects.

2 Place the pointer at one corner of this rectangle.

3 Drag the broken outline to enclose them all.

4 Release the mouse button and check that all have acquired handles.

# Selecting for Cut and Copy

These techniques should work with most Windows application. Some will also offer additional selection methods of their own, which may be more convenient in some situations.

You normally select **text** by dragging the pointer over the desired block of characters.

The highlight shows the selected text.

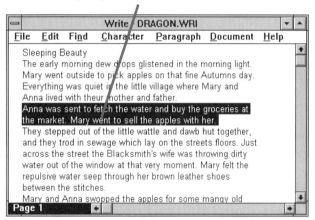

With DTP, or other applications that work with **objects** – including the cells of spreadsheets and tables – you select a single object by clicking on it, or a group of objects by dragging an outline around them all.

Selected objects are usually indicated by handles.

The enclosing outline

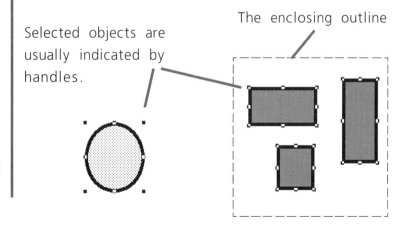

# Copying the screen

When a PC is working in DOS mode pressing **[Print Screen]** will send a copy of the screen directly to the printer. When you are working in Windows, the copy goes to the Clipboard. This gives you the chance to edit it before printing, or to pass it on to an application.

Press **[Print Screen]** to copy the entire screen.

Press **[Alt]-[Print Screen]** to copy the active window.

The screen snapshot can then be pasted directly into a suitable application – a graphics or DTP package, or a word-processor that can handle graphics. If you want to edit it first, paste it into Paintbrush. (See Section 12.) The screen samples in this book were all produced by capturing the screen or window, and trimming off unwanted parts in Paintbrush.

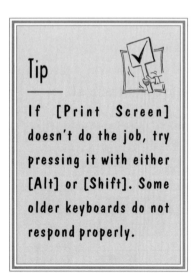

**Tip**

If **[Print Screen]** doesn't do the job, try pressing it with either **[Alt]** or **[Shift]**. Some older keyboards do not respond properly.

# Basic steps

❑ **Copying the screen**

1 Tidy up the screen, removing or minimising unwanted windows, and arranging the others to focus your message clearly.

2 Press **[Print Screen]**.

3 Move to the application into which you want to insert the snapshot, or to Paintbrush.

4 Open the **Edit** menu and **Paste**.

❑ **Copying a window**

1 Adjust the size of the window to fit text or image you want to display.

2 Hold **[Alt]** and press **[Print Screen]**.

3 **Paste** the snapshot into the target application.

# The clipboard viewer

## Basic steps

❑ **Clearing the Clipboard**

1 Open the Clipboard Viewer.

2 Open the Edit menu and click **Delete** or press **[Delete]**.

3 Press **OK** when asked to confirm the clearance.

❑ **Saving a Clipboard file**

1 Don't.

2 Paste it into Paintbrush and save it from there in a sensible format.

This is to be found in the Main group. It will let you see what is in the Clipboard, clear the contents, and save the contents as a file – or load it from a file. In practice, there is only one thing that it can do which cannot be done as well or better by other applications.

When Windows copies a graphic into the Clipboard, it does so in a variety of formats - all at once. As a result, it takes a lot more memory than you might expect. The picture of the icon at the top of this page can be stored in 2047 bytes as a PCX file, 4830 as a bitmap, or 21741 as a Clipboard file. A second aspect of this multi-format storage is that only the Clipboard can use Clipboard files. So..

If you Windows ever warns you that it is running short of memory, the first thing you should do is to clear the Clipboard. This is best done from the Viewer.

If you want to save a Cut graphic, do not use the Clipboard's Save command, with its CLP format. Paste it into Paintbrush and save it as a BMP or PCX file.

① Open the Viewer

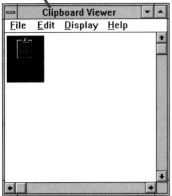

② Choose Edit | Delete

③ Yes please

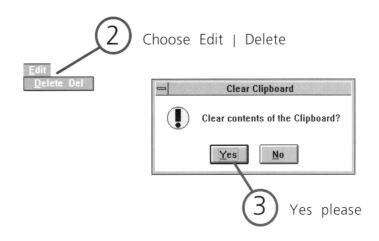

# The character map

Character Map

This shows the full set of characters that are present in any given font, and allows you to select one or more individual characters for copying into other applications. Its main use is probably for picking up Wingdings for decoration, or the odd foreign letter or mathematical symbols in otherwise straight text.

The characters are rather small, but you can get a better look at a character, by holding the mouse button down while you point at it. This produces a double-size image.

**Basic steps**

1 Go to Program Manager and select **Character Map**.

2 Select the **Font**.

3 Click on the character you want to highlight it.

4 Click **Select** to copy it to the **Character to Copy** slot.

5 Go back over 3 and 4 as necessary.

6 Click **Copy**.

7 **Paste** them back into your application.

(2) Select the Font

(3) Highlight a character

(4) Click Select

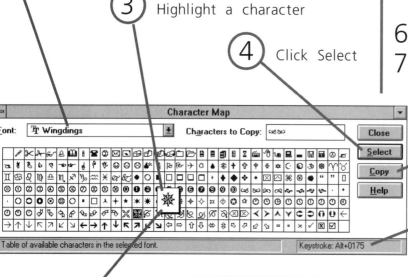

(6) Click Copy

Note the keystroke

Hold down the button to magnify

**Tip**

If you are going to use a character often, learn its keystroke. This is shown at the bottom right. For Alt+ ones, hold **[Alt]** and type the number on the **Number Pad**.

# Basic steps

PIF Editor

1   Go to Program Manager and run the **PIF Editor**.

2   Pull down the **File** menu and select **Open**.

3   Select the *.pif* file with the same name as the program.

4   Check the memory settings with the program's manual.

5   Set the **Display Usage** to **Windowed** if you want to integrate this program with other Windows software.

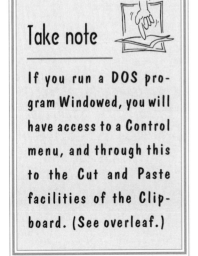
# Editing a PIF

When you install a DOS program and add it to a group, Windows will create a PIF file (Program Information File) that determines how the program works. The default settings are usually very good and should be left alone as long as all is well. If you find that the program does not work properly under Windows, try adjusting the settings, using the PIF editor.

Are the Program Filename (including its path) and the Start-up directory correct?

How many Kb of memory does it Require or Desire?

Does it need Expanded (EMS) or Extended (XMS) Memory, and how much?

The program's manual should give you this information.

```
┌─────────────────────────────────────────────────────┐
│ ─          PIF Editor - QBASIC.PIF            ▼ ▲    │
│  File   Mode   Help                                  │
│  Program Filename:    c:\dos\qbasic.exe              │
│  Window Title:        Microsoft QBASIC               │
│  Optional Parameters:                                │
│  Start-up Directory:  c:\dos                         │
│  Video Memory:   ● Text  ○ Low Graphics  ○ High Graphics │
│  Memory Requirements:  KB Required [330] KB Desired [640] │
│  EMS Memory:       KB Required [0]  KB Limit [0]     │
│  XMS Memory:       KB Required [0]  KB Limit [0]     │
│  Display Usage: ● Full Screen    Execution: ☐ Background │
│                 ○ Windowed                  ☐ Exclusive │
│  ☒ Close Window on Exit    [ Advanced... ]           │
│  Press F1 for Help on Program Filename.              │
└─────────────────────────────────────────────────────┘
```

# MS-DOS prompt

## Basic steps

This gives you the standard C:> prompt, from which you can run any DOS utility or application. Use it if you are having trouble running a DOS program as an item, or if you want to use it so rarely that it is not worth the bother of bringing it into Windows.

Make sure that you can get to the Control menu. Either use the PIF editor to set its **Display Usage** to **Windowed** (page 121), or use the **Properties** dialog box to set it to **Run Minimised** ( page 54).

❏ **Changing the Settings**

1 Open the **Control menu** by clicking the top left button, or the minimised icon.

2 Select **Settings**.

3 Check that the **Display Option** is set to **Window**.

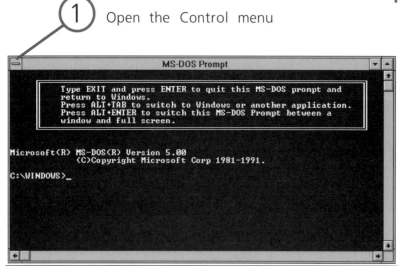

(1) Open the Control menu

Take note

When you have done with the MS-DOS prompt, type **EXIT** to close it down.

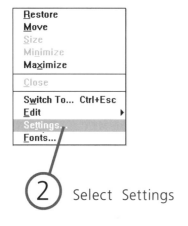

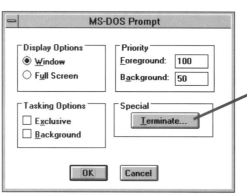

(2) Select Settings

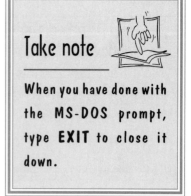

You can use this to force an immediate end to the MS-DOS prompt.

# Basic steps

## ❏ Copying

1 Open the Control menu.

2 Select **Edit**, then **Mark**.

3 Highlight the text you want to copy.

4 Open the Control menu again and select **Edit | Copy**.

5 Switch to your target application and paste the text there.

## ❏ Pasting

1 Copy text from your source application into the Clipboard.

2 Switch to the DOS application, and place the cursor where you want the text to go.

3 Open the Control menu and select **Edit | Paste**.

# Copy and Paste in MS-DOS

The most useful item on the menu is Edit. With this you can copy text between DOS and Windows applications. Copying is slightly different than in Windows as you must first use **Edit | Mark** to highlight the block of text. To do this, imagine a rectangle that encloses the text you want to copy. Point to one corner of this and drag the highlight to the opposite corner.

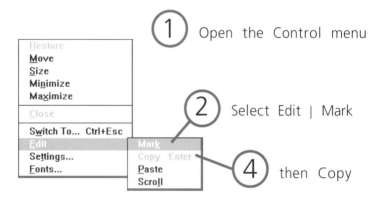

The **Fonts** option on the Control menu lets you choose the size of text that is used in the MS-DOS window. The window's size varies with the font size, so that it holds the same quantity of text. The **Preview** shows the size of the window relative to the whole screen.

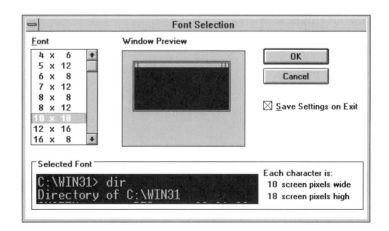

# Summary

❑ The **Clipboard** is used for copying text and images within and between documents.

❑ Text can be selected by dragging a highlight over it.

❑ Individual objects can be selected by clicking on them. Groups of objects can usually bve selected by dragging outlines around them.

❑ An image of the screen can be copied to the Clipboard by pressing **[Print Screen]**. An image of the active window can be copied by pressing [Alt]-[Print Screen].

❑ The **Clipboard viewer** displays whatever is currently in the Clipboard.

❑ If the Clipboard holds a large graphic, clearing it can free up a lot of valuable memory.

❑ The **PIF Editor** lets you adjust the settings for DOS programs that have been brought into Windows.

❑ If DOS programs, or the **MS-DOS prompt,** are run in a window, you have access to the Control menu, and through this to the Clipboard's Copy and Paste facilities.

# 12 Words and Pictures

# Starting to Write

Write is the Windows word-processor. For a freebie it is remarkably good, offering a better range of facilities than many commercial offerings of just a few years ago. Its features include:

- good editing facilities

- a full range of fonts and sizes

- control of line spacing and alignment

- tabs and indents

- imported graphics, graphs, tables and text.

To get started, you can simply begin typing as soon as the window opens, but it is often better to turn on the ruler and set the layout first.

## Basic steps

1 Open the **Document** menu.

2 Select **Ruler On**.

3 Select **Layout**.

4 In the **Layout** dialog box, check and adjust the size of the margins. (Note the choice of inch or cm measurements.)

5 Click **OK**.

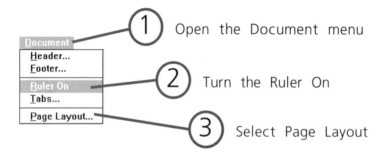

1 Open the Document menu

2 Turn the Ruler On

3 Select Page Layout

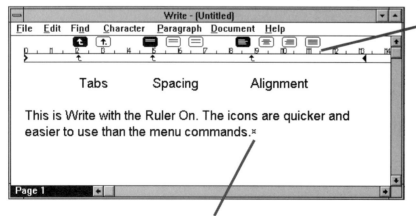

The **Ruler** controls the position of the tabs and the left and right idents. It also has icons that offer an easy way to set line spacing and text alignment.

The star marks the end of the text

# Basic steps

## Adding a Header

1 Open the **Document** menu.

2 Select **Header**.

3 At the dialog box, set the **Distance from top**, and click the check box if you want to **Print on First Page**.

4 In the main window, type the text that you want to appear.

5 If you want to include the page number, click on **Insert Page #**.

6 **Return to Document** when done.

❏ You can go back over the same routine to edit the header later.

❏ Footers are added in exactly the same way.

# The Layout

This option on the **Document** menu is used to set the size of the margins, and the numbering of the pages.

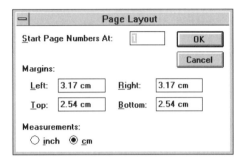

## Headers and footers

These can be added at any time, not just at the start. When the Page Header (or Footer) dialog box is open, type the header text into the main window. It will disappear when you return to the document, but will be there when you print.

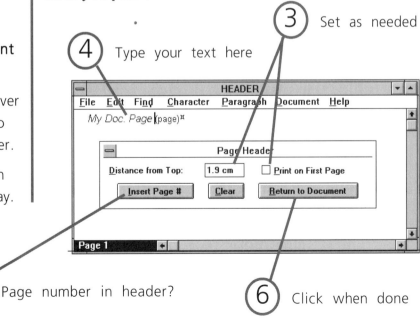

③ Set as needed

④ Type your text here

⑤ Page number in header?

⑥ Click when done

# Editing and styling text

When you start a new file, you will see two items at the top left of the window. The flashing bar | is the text cursor – i.e., wherever this is, is where text will appear when you type. The small star ⊐ marks the end of the text. You cannot move beyond or below this.

● To move the text cursor, either use the arrow keys or point with the mouse and click.

● To delete single characters, either press ⬅ Backspace to delete the one to the left of the text cursor, or [Delete] to remove the one to the right.

● To delete a block of text, highlight it with the mouse and press [Delete].

When entering text, note that Write has a **wordwrap** feature. This means that you just keep typing when you reach the end of a line and Write takes the word down to the next line. You only press [Enter] when you want to end a paragraph. By typing a paragraph as a continuous stream, you ensure that it stays together if you change the font size or the page width.

Tip

Don't forget that you can use **Edit ICut, Copy** and **Paste** for moving blocks of text.

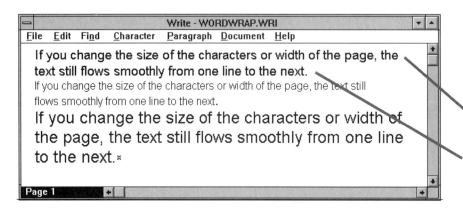

Don't press [Enter] at the end of a line – only at the end of the paragraph.

# Basic steps

1 If you want to format an existing block of text, highlight it first.

2 Open the **Character** menu.

3 Select the effect or **Fonts** to change the typeface.

4 In the **Fonts** dialog box, select the **Font** before turning to the **Style** and **Size**.

# Fonts and styles

Write gives you access to the full range of fonts styles, sizes and typefaces that are present on your system. Set these before you start to type and all subsequent text will appear in the format, or highlight a block of existing text and change its style.

The font styles are reached through the **Character** menu.

**Bold**, *italic*, <u>underline</u>, subscript and superscript are all toggle switches – click to turn the effect on, or to turn it off.

Enlarge and reduce pull the character size up or down a couple of points. You can resize the same block of text several times to enlarge or reduce it further.

To change the typeface, use the **Fonts** option, and select from the dialog box. The Sample pane is very useful when you are searching for the right effect.

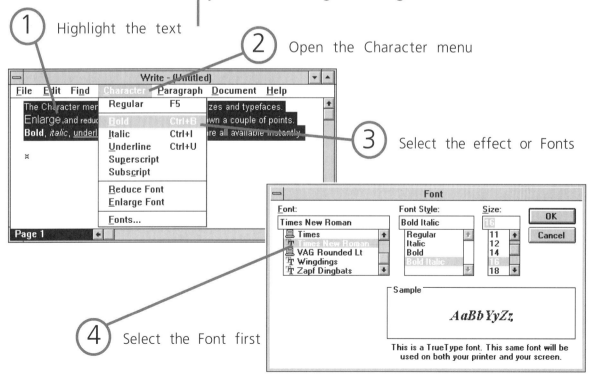

Highlight the text

Open the Character menu

Select the effect or Fonts

Select the Font first

# Formatting paragraphs

The alignment of text – whether it sits up against the Left or Right, or both edges, or in the Centre, the line spacing and the indents from the edges are controlled from the Paragraph menu, or more simply from the Ruler. The Ruler is also used for setting tabs. All of these can be set at the start to apply to the whole document, or later to format selected paragraphs.

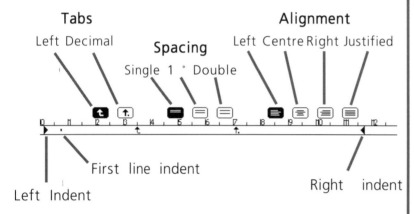

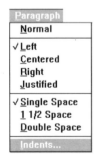

The Paragraph menu duplicates the Ruler, though the dialog box does allow more accurate positioning of Indents.

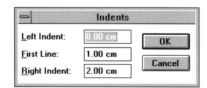

# Alignment

**Left** aligned text has 'ragged edges' on the right – use it for less formal text and in narrow columns.

**Centre** alignment is useful for picking out items.

**Right** alignment is often used for addresses on letters

**Justified** text is aligned to both edges, and can leave large gaps in the text.

# Indents

Indents push the text in from the Margins (set in the **Document | Page Layout** routine).

Drag the ▶ triangles ◀ to set the indents.

You can also set a **First line indent** by dragging the dot along the Ruler.

# Saving and opening files

1 Open the **File** menu.

2 Select **Save As** with a new file, or to save a file under a new name. Select **Save** to resave an existing file.

3 At the **Save As** dialog box, select the **Drive/ Directory**.

4 Change the **File Type** if you don't want to use the WRI format.

5 Type in a filename – don't bother to type the .WRI (or other) extension. This is added automatically.

6 Click **OK**.

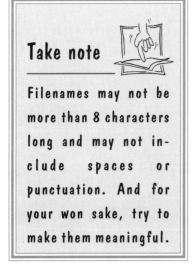

## Take note

Filenames may not be more than 8 characters long and may not in- clude spaces or punctuation. And for your won sake, try to make them meaningful.

## Saving

Write can save files in several formats, which can be very useful. If the document is only going to be used inWrite, or in other Windows applications, then stick to the de- fault Write format (WRI). This saves the layout and font settings as well as the text. If you want to be able to transfer it to Word for DOS, you can either keep the layout and font styles (DOC) or save it as Text Only. The plain Text file type will transfer to almost any word-processor.

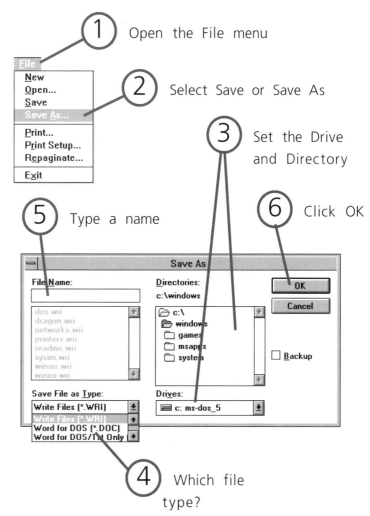

① Open the File menu

② Select Save or Save As

③ Set the Drive and Directory

⑤ Type a name

⑥ Click OK

④ Which file type?

# Opening files

Write will happily handle Word for DOS and plain text files as well as those saved in its own file type. It will even have a bash at files from other word-processors, though the results are likely to be unpredictable as the formatting codes will not be translated.

When opening text files into Write, you will be asked whether or not you want to convert to Write format. Some files are best left as plain text. If you are editing your AUTOEXEC.BAT or CONFIG.SYS or any INI file (the ones that hold INItial settings for programs), these must be left as text. When in doubt, don't convert.

## Basic steps

1 Open the **File** menu.

2 Select **Open**.

3 At the dialog box, set the **Drive/Directory**.

4 Change the **File Type** if it is not a Write file.

5 Select the file from the list.

6 Click **OK**.

7 With text files you will be offered a Conversion option. Accept it only if you need to convert.

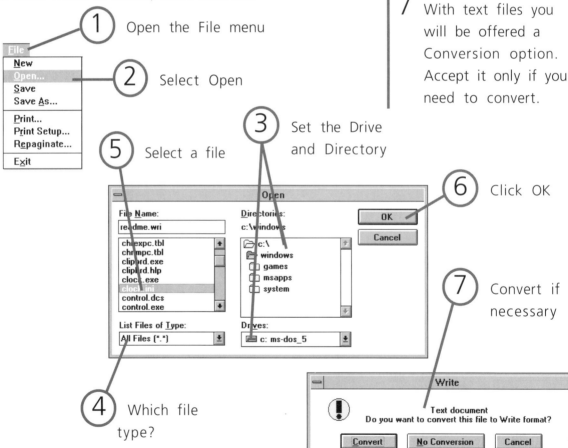

1 Open the File menu

2 Select Open

3 Set the Drive and Directory

5 Select a file

6 Click OK

7 Convert if necessary

4 Which file type?

File menu:
New
Open...
Save
Save As...
Print...
Print Setup...
Repaginate...
Exit

Open dialog:
File Name: readme.wri
chiexpc.tbl
chrmpc.tbl
cliprd.exe
cliprd.hlp
clock.exe
clock.ini
control.dcs
control.exe
List Files of Type: All Files [*.*]
Directories: c:\windows
c:\
windows
games
msapps
system
Drives: c: ms-dos_5
OK
Cancel

Write:
Text document
Do you want to convert this file to Write format?
Convert    No Conversion    Cancel

# Basic steps

## Graphics in Write

To import a picture

1 Run **Paintbrush** and open or create a drawing.

2 Select the image and **Copy** it.

3 Return to **Write**.

4 Place the cursor on a blank line above or below your text.

5 Open the **Edit** menu and select **Paste**.

> **For Paintbrush, see pages 136 to 141.**

## Importing pictures

Write can handle graphics to a limited extent. It is not DTP, but at least you can mix pictures and text. The main limitation is that a graphic must sit on a line by itself – you cannot run text by the side of it.

The simplest way to import a picture is to use the Clipboard to copy it in from Paintbrush or another graphics package. Once in place, the picture can be moved or resized, and if necessary, you can call up the graphics package and edit it from within Write.

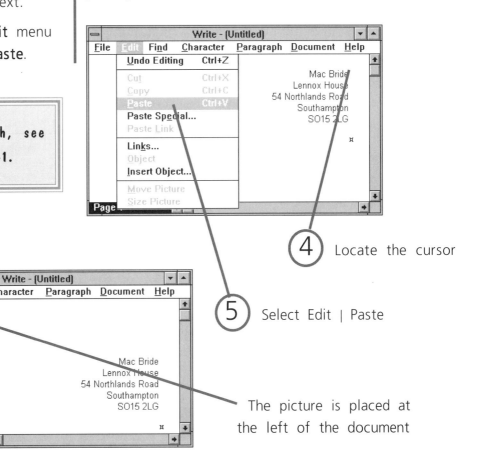

④ Locate the cursor

⑤ Select Edit | Paste

The picture is placed at the left of the document

## Editing a picture

One of the treats of Windows is the way that applications can be linked together. You can see this in Write when you want to edit a picture. Simply double-clicking on it, or clicking once and selecting Edit Picture Object, will call up Paintbrush and load your picture into it.

## Moving a picture

Forget what I said earlier about what a selected object looks like in Windows. Write pictures are different! You select – as usual – by clicking on them. When selected a picture is highlighted, and when you are moving or resizing, there is a grey outline – there are no handles.

Movement is limited to left and right. If you want to change the vertical position of the picture, you must add or delete lines above it.

Forget about the usual dragging actions as well. In Write, you only press the mouse button when you want to drop the picture in its new place.

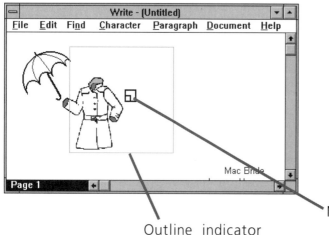

Outline indicator

Move/Size picture cursor

❏ **To edit a picture**

1 Click on the picture to highlight it.

2 Open the **Edit** menu and select **Edit Paintbrush Picture Object**.

3 Paintbrush will start up, with the picture ready for editing.

4 When you have done, open Paintbrush's **File** menu and select **Exit and Return**.

❏ **To move a picture**

1 Click to select the picture.

2 Open the **Edit** menu and select **Move Picture**.

3 Keeping your fingers off the buttons, move the mouse to pull the outline left or right.

4 Click to set the picture in its new position.

# Basic steps

1 Select the picture.

2 Open the **Edit** menu.

3 Select **Size Picture**

4 Move the cursor to an edge then keep moving to pull the edge to a new position.

5 If necessary, slide the cursor around the outline to another edge.

6 When you are satified, click the left mouse button.

## Tip

If you want accurate scaling, keep an eye on the X, Y scale factors at the bottom left.

# Changing the size

The technique here is also unlike any you will meet elsewhere in Windows. When you first get into the Size routine, the square cursor will be in the middle of the outline. Move the mouse – don't drag – to an edge or corner. When you get there, the cursor will connect, without you doing anything, and further movement will pull the outline to a new size.

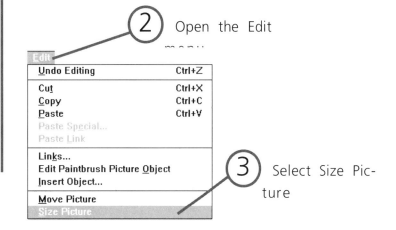

② Open the Edit menu

③ Select Size Picture

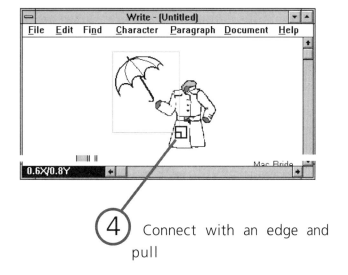

④ Connect with an edge and pull

# Paintbrush

Like Write, Paintbrush is excellent value for a freebie. I wouldn't want to draw house plans or paint a landscape with it, but it has all that's needed to produce illustrations for reports or fun pictures for kids of all ages. You can also load in and edit screenshots, BMP (bitmap) or PCX files from other graphics software or from a scanner.

The main working area normally extends beyond the visible screen – it is big enough to fill an A4 sheet of paper when printed. To its left is a set of **Tools** with a selection of **Line thickness** below, and across the bottom is your **Palette** of colours. The meaning of the colour indicator varies. Most of the time the outer colour is the background, and the inner is the paint; with filled shapes, the outer refers to the outline , and the inner to the fill colour.

All selections are by clicking the left button, it is the right button to select the background colour.

## Basic steps

❑ Starting a new picture

1 Right click on a colour to select the background colour.

2 Open the **File** menu and select **New**.

3 Left click a colour to select you first paint.

4 Select your first Tool.

5 Give your creativity free rein.

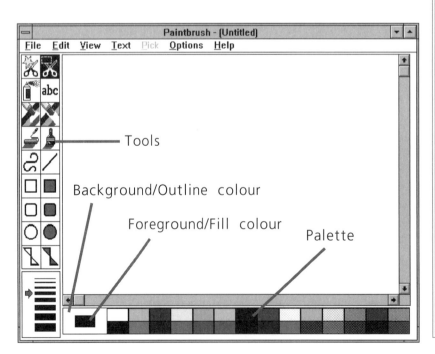

Tools

Background/Outline colour

Foreground/Fill colour

Palette

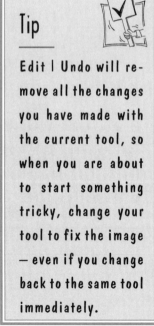

## Tip

Edit I Undo will remove all the changes you have made with the current tool, so when you are about to start something tricky, change your tool to fix the image – even if you change back to the same tool immediately.

# The Tools

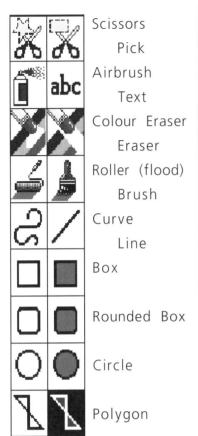

| | | |
|---|---|---|
| | | Scissors |
| | | Pick |
| | | Airbrush |
| | | Text |
| | | Colour Eraser |
| | | Eraser |
| | | Roller (flood) |
| | | Brush |
| | | Curve |
| | | Line |
| | | Box |
| | | Rounded Box |
| | | Circle |
| | | Polygon |

**Scissors** and **Pick** are both used to select an area of the screen – Scissors by freehand drawing, Pick by dragging a rectangular outline. The selected area can then be Cut or Copied, or manipulated with the **Pick** menu options.

With **Text**, click to position the text cursor then type. You can change the **Font** (using the menu options) or colour of the text before, during or after you have typed. It is only fixed when you pick a new tool, or reposition the cursor to start a new line of text.

The **Colour Eraser** replaces anything in the current foreground colour with the background colour. It can therefore either wipe out unwanted items or recolour them.

The **Roller** floods an area with the current foreground colour. The area must have a solid outline, or the paint will leak out and cover more than you intended. (Be ready to use **Edit | Undo** whenever you get the Roller out.)

All lines and shapes are drawn by dragging a thin, adjustable line. As soon as you release the mouse button, the permanent drawing is painted onto the screen.

**Curves** are tricky to get right. Start be dragging a straight line from one end to the other. If you want a simple curve, go back and drag the middle of the line to bend it, then click at either end to fix the shape. For a double bend, drag the line to get the first curve, then drag it again from another point for the second. The shape is fixed when you release the button the second time.

With the **Polygons**, drag each line in turn to make the shape. It is only completed when you drag a line back to meet the startpoint.

**Take note**

The thickness of all lines, outlines and of the Airbrush nozzle is controlled by clicking on a sample Line in the box at the bottom left.

# Close Ups

Few people can work accurately with a mouse, but we can **Zoom In** close to our paintings to tidy up jagged edges and add other finishing touches. In this mode, the pixels (dots) are represented as squares, big enough to handle. The only tools you have are the Brush, which colours one pixel at a time, and the Roller, which floods the area up to a differently coloured boundary or the edge of the screen. You also have Edit | Undo, which cancels all the changes you have made since first zooming in.

If you are working on a picture that is bigger than the window, **Zoom Out** will give you an overview.

## Basic steps

1　Open the **View** menu.

2　Select **Zoom In**.

3　Move the outline to the area you want to magnify and click.

4　When you have done, open the **View** menu and select **Zoom Out**.

### Tip

You can soften jagged lines by adding dots of a lighter shade.

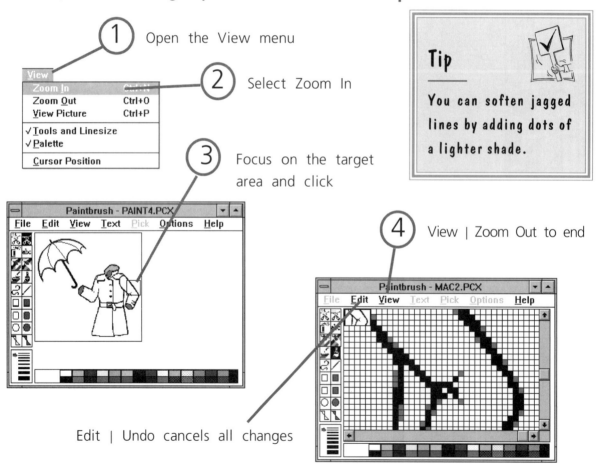

① Open the View menu

② Select Zoom In

③ Focus on the target area and click

④ View | Zoom Out to end

Edit | Undo cancels all changes

# Basic steps

# Paintbrush options

❑ **Setting Attributes**

1 Open the **Options** menu.

2 Select **Image Attributes**.

3 At the dialog box, set the size of the image, and the colour mode.

4 Click **OK** to fix the settings. They will take effect when you start a new picture.

❑ **Editing Colours**

1 Double click on a colour in the Palette.

2 At the **Edit Colors** dialog box, drag or click beside the sliders to adjust the Red, Green, Blue components of the colour.

3 Click **OK** to place the adjusted colour back in the Palette.

4 If desired, use **Options | Save Palette** to store the colours as a PAL file.

The **Image Attributes** sets the size of the working area, and allows you to select Colour or Black and White. If you know in advance how large you want the image to be, you can set the size exactly. If the image is relatively small, and will be incorporated into a DTP'd report and output to laser or other high-definition printer, you would do better to set the working area two or three times as large. It can then be scaled down, and will give a crisper image, as there are more dots per inch on a laser printer than there are pixels per inch on most screens.

Colours can be edited from this menu, or by double-clicking on the Palette. The customised palette can then be saved and reloaded from this menu.

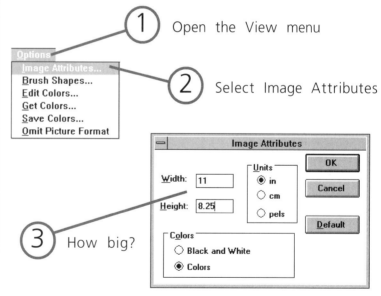

① Open the View menu

② Select Image Attributes

③ How big?

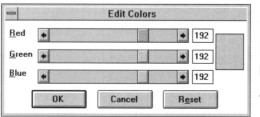

You are mixing light, not paint. More colour makes a paler shade.

# Selected areas

You can select a fragment of the screen with either Scissors ✂ or Pick ✂. Once selected, the area can then be Cut or Copied, but it can also be dragged to a new place, or transformed with the options on the **Pick** menu.

The two **Flips** both produce mirror images to replace the original. **Inverse** similarly replaces the original with a 'negative' of itself. **Shrink + Grow** and **Tilt** work with copies. You drag an outline, and when you release the mouse button, a scaled or tilted copy is placed on screen.

Scaling and tilting

1 Use the **Pick** tool to select an area. If you misjudge it, click somewhere else on screen to cancel and start again.

2 Open the **Pick** menu.

3 Select **Shrink + Grow** or **Tilt**.

4 Drag an outline to the required size and shape.

5 Release the mouse button.

6 Repeat as often as necessary.

7 When you have done, click a new Tool.

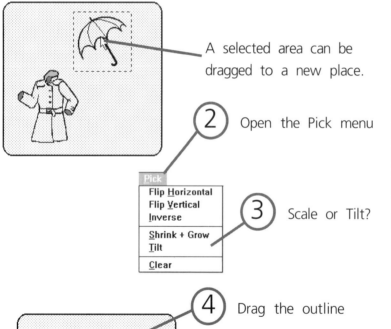

A selected area can be dragged to a new place.

2 Open the Pick menu

| Pick |
| --- |
| Flip **H**orizontal |
| Flip **V**ertical |
| **I**nverse |
| **S**hrink + Grow |
| **T**ilt |
| **C**lear |

3 Scale or Tilt?

4 Drag the outline

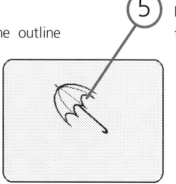

5 Release to get a transformed copy

**140**

## Basic steps

1 Click on the **Pick** tool and drag an outline around the area you want to save.

2 Open the **Edit** menu.

3 It should now contain the **Copy To** option. Select it.

4 At the **Copy To** dialog box, set the drive and directory, select the right file type and give the file a name.

# Saving pictures

Paintbrush can output files in PCX or BMP formats, with the bitmaps ranging, in order of detail (and filesize) from monochrome to 24-bit colour. What sort you should use depends largely upon what application yuo will be passing the pictures to. PCX files are compact but accurate, and are often the best choice though some applications work better with bitmaps.

The whole of the current picture can be saved with the **Save** or **Save As** option on the **File** menu, but there may well be times when you do not want the whole of it. That's no problem, as you can easily save a selected area.

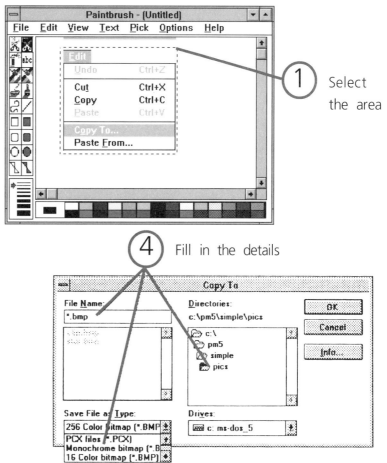

① Select the area

② Open the Edit menu

③ Select Copy To

④ Fill in the details

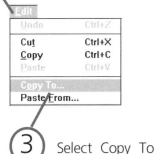

# Summary

❏ **Write** is a good, basic wordprocessor with all the features you need to cope with most tasks.

❏ The **Page Layout** and **Margins** should be set before you start. **Headers** and **Footers** can be added then, or at any later time.

❏ Having the **Ruler** visible makes it easier to set Tabs, Indents, Alignment and Spacing.

❏ A full range of **Fonts**, styles and sizes is available.

❏ Write can save and open files in Write, Word for DOS and plain Text formats.

❏ **Graphics** can be Pasted into documents, and their size and position adjusted.

❏ **Paintbrush** offers a range of **Tools** for drawing, colouring and adding text.

❏ You can set the size of the working area and edit the colours in the Paintbrush **Palette**.

❏ Selected areas of the screen can be copied, manipulated using the **Pick** options, or saved to disk.

# Basic steps

1 Go to Program Manager and run **Windows Setup**.

2 Pull down the **Options** menu.

3 Select **Add/Remove Windows Components**.

4 Work through each of the others in turn, clicking on the **Files** button.

5 Click on each unwanted item in the right hand pane. Click again to deselect if you make a mistake.

6 Click **Remove** to transfer them to the left hand pane.

7 Click **OK** to start the removals – you will be asked to confirm, so there is a chance to change your mind.

# Slimming Windows

If you could do with a little more space on your hard disk, it is worth clearing out those accessories and other peripherals that you do not use. There are almost 2.5 Mb of optional components, and you will probably find that the ones you don't use add up to around 1Mb. Few of us use all the accessories; you only need one screen saver and one wallpaper pattern; the WAV sound files are only of use if you have a sound card; and we are all agreed that the games are just a waste of time – aren't we?

Removing unwanted items is easy, and it is just as easy to put them back later if you decide they are needed.

Run Windows Setup

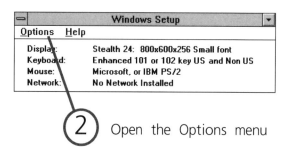

Open the Options menu

③ Select Add/Remove Windows Components

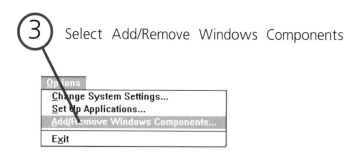

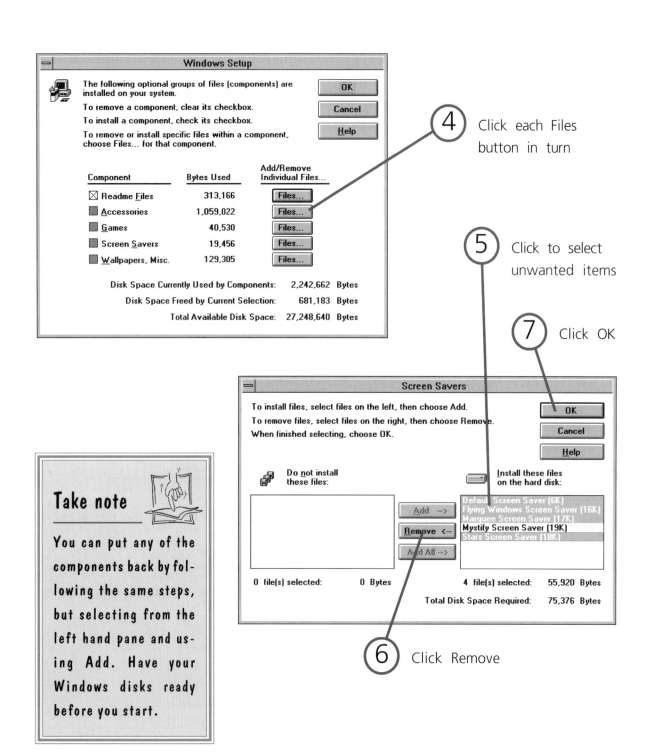

**Windows Setup**

The following optional groups of files (components) are installed on your system.

To remove a component, clear its checkbox.

To install a component, check its checkbox.

To remove or install specific files within a component, choose Files... for that component.

OK

Cancel

Help

④ Click each Files button in turn

| Component | Bytes Used | Add/Remove Individual Files... |
|---|---|---|
| ☒ Readme Files | 313,166 | Files... |
| ▨ Accessories | 1,059,022 | Files... |
| ▨ Games | 40,530 | Files... |
| ▨ Screen Savers | 19,456 | Files... |
| ▨ Wallpapers, Misc. | 129,305 | Files... |

Disk Space Currently Used by Components: 2,242,662 Bytes

Disk Space Freed by Current Selection: 681,183 Bytes

Total Available Disk Space: 27,248,640 Bytes

⑤ Click to select unwanted items

⑦ Click OK

**Screen Savers**

To install files, select files on the left, then choose Add.

To remove files, select files on the right, then choose Remove.

When finished selecting, choose OK.

OK

Cancel

Help

Do not install these files:

Install these files on the hard disk:

Add -->

Remove <--

Add All -->

Default Screen Saver (6K)
Flying Windows Screen Saver (16K)
Marquee Screen Saver (17K)
**Mystify Screen Saver (19K)**
Stars Screen Saver (18K)

0 file(s) selected:    0 Bytes

4 file(s) selected:    55,920 Bytes

Total Disk Space Required:    75,376 Bytes

⑥ Click Remove

**Take note**

You can put any of the components back by following the same steps, but selecting from the left hand pane and using Add. Have your Windows disks ready before you start.

# Index